Make Up Your Mind to Live or Die

Poems of Love and Sorrow resulting from Lost Love and Lost Health

Conrad Birmingham

L W Birmingham and Sons LLC

Copy Right © 2021 L W Birmingham and Sons LLC

L W Birmingham and Sons LLC

Scripture is taken from the Holy Bible, New International Version ®. Copyright © 1973, 1978, 1984 by International Bible Society. Used by permission of Zondervan Publishing House. All rights reserved.

This is a work of fiction. Names, characters, places, and incidents either are the products of the author's imagination or are used fictitiously. Any resemblance to actual persons living or dead, businesses, companies, events, or locales is entirely coincidental.

The characters and events portrayed in this book are fictitious. Any similarity to real persons, living or dead, is coincidental and not intended by the author.

Although the author and publisher have made every effort to ensure that the in-formation in this book was correct at press time, the author and publisher do not assume and at this moment disclaim any liability to any party for any loss, dam-age, or disruption caused by errors or omissions, whether such errors or omissions result from negligence, accident, or any other cause.

No part of this book may be reproduced, or stored in a retrieval system, or trans-mitted in any form or by any means, electronic, mechanical, photocopying, re-cording, or otherwise, without express written© permission of the publisher.

I dedicate this book to my friend, Cynthia Thomson. The majority of the poems are about her and our relationship.

Proverbs 1:7 Start with God—the first step in learning is bowing down to God; only fools thumb their noses at such wisdom and learning.

Proverbs 1:20-21 Lady Wisdom goes out in the street and shouts. At the town center she makes her speech.
In the middle of the traffic she takes her stand. At the busiest corner she calls out:

Proverbs 1:22-24 "Simpletons! How long will you wallow in ignorance? Cynics! How long will you feed your cynicism?
Idiots! How long will you refuse to learn? About face! I can revise your life. Look, I'm ready to pour out my spirit on you; I'm ready to tell you all I know. As it is, I've called, but you've turned a deaf ear; I've reached out to you, but you've ignored me.

Proverbs 1:25-28 "Since you laugh at my counsel and make a joke of my advice, How can I take you seriously? I'll turn the tables and joke about your troubles! What if the roof falls in, and your whole life goes to pieces? What if catastrophe strikes and there's nothing to show for your life but rubble and ashes? You'll need me then. You'll call for me, but don't expect an answer. No matter how hard you look, you won't find me.

Proverbs 1:29-33 "Because you hated Knowledge and had nothing to do with the Fear-of-God,
Because you wouldn't take my advice and brushed aside all my offers to train you,
Well, you've made your bed—now lie in it; you wanted your own way—now, how do you like it? Don't you see what happens, you simpletons, you idiots? Carelessness kills; complacency is murder.

First pay attention to me, and then relax. Now you can take it easy—you're in good hands."

The Message Bible

Table of Contents

Preface 10
Introduction 12
    Why I Write 12
    Senseless Crap 13
    Punctuation 15
Chapter 1 - Birthdays and Holidays 17
    Birthdays 19
        My Birthday 19
        Sweet Number Seven 22
        Little Birthday Girl 24
        Birthday Again 27
        College Dorm Birthdays 29
    Holidays 31
        Memorial Day 31
        Easter 33
        Halloween 36
        Valentines 39
        My Patriot Song 42
        Christmas 46
Chapter 2 - Politics and Issues of 2020 51
    Election 53
    Feel 59
    Global Warming 62

When Do You Live	65
Persecution	67
Children Of Men	73
Election Debate	82
Immigration	86
Taxes	89
Woke Culture	93
All Lives Matter	96
Chapter 3 - What Makes Me Tick	**99**
Bible	102
Disappointed	104
Checklist	107
My Dance	110
Remember	114
Torment	118
Bore	122
Chapter 4 - Family and Friends	**124**
Be A Friend	126
Daughter	127
Family	129
Atlanta	133
Speed Dating	136
People In Your Life	142
George Harrison	146
Dale Treadway	148

Jim Linberg 151
Chapter 5 - Love 156
    Leigh 157
    Love 161
    I Am What I Am 163
    Love Grows 164
    Adore 166
    Sailing the Lee 176
    All About Today 179
    Marriage 183
Chapter 6 – Grief and Sorrow 196
    Heart Ache 198
    Done 201
    Grateful 203
    Grief to Life 207
    Change 213
    Retreat and Rout 217
    Revelation 222
    Darkness than Light 225
    Ferocious Tide 229
    Hope and Expectations 234
    Night to Day 237
Chapter 7 - My Health 241
    Battle of Nerves vs Medical 243
    The Drug 246

It is the Season	249
Just Write	252
Doctors	254
My Heart	258
Chapter 8 - My Fourth Quarter	261
End of Game	263
Fall Apart	266
Never Too Late	268
Epilogue	272
About the Author	273
Books By the Author	275

Preface

I am sharing my second book of poems. A continuation of my journey through life-fighting illnesses, enjoying friendships, loving a woman, managing anxiety, reminiscing of past experiences, worshiping God, and contemplating the craziness of the past election.

I did not include questions and scripture after each poem. Most of the reviews and comments about Uplifting Poems About the Death of a Loved One were hostile toward the questions but predominantly antagonistic about the Bible scripture. I left out the Bible scripture for this reason. I would rather people read my poems with

elements of God present than to have a negative connotation about my poetry because of the scripture included after each verse,

All of my poems are included and updated in my book, Conrad Birmingham: Mini-book with My Seekers Help Me Believe Lessons, Blog Posts, Novels, and Mini-Book Writings. This book is an anthology of all my writings which will be updated free as I write and add material.

I continue to work on a novel, but it is challenging when I take the drug Amitriptyline. I cannot read or write. I cannot create meaningful thoughts that I can put on paper. There are a few poems that highlight this dilemma.

Battle of Nerves vs Medical

The Drug

I hope you enjoy these poems about my medical condition and the other verses.

Introduction

Why do I have anything to say, or you know your poems are awful are the two things that I hear the most, especially from my friends. Can you believe your friends are the ones who criticize you the most? I added these poems in the introduction about why I write poetry. I hope you enjoy or understand me better.

Why I Write

Why write verse
Why share your views
Why live a curse
Why parade your blues

I have things to say
And so do you
The American way
Since our first coup

You may disagree
You may squirm
You may flee
You may confirm

But here we are
Sharing our ideologies
Not to yell or spar
Or to give apologies

But to be true
And frank
Knowledge to pursue
Sort of a plank

Explaining my positions
Explaining my thoughts
Explaining my decisions
Explaining my brain knots

The verse facilitates
It helps me to recall
Poetry opens the gates
When I hit a blank wall

To eliminate the haziness
The clutter from medications
To lesson my craziness
And the accompanying frustrations

That is why I write
To express my thoughts
And to feel right
I hope this connected the dots

Senseless Crap

My poetry is crap
Who cares
Not memorable rap
Do not split hairs

Senseless
Personal triviality
Defenseless
Lacking emotionality

In defense
These are my thoughts
My two cents
I connect my dots

How did I get here
Where am I going
No Shakespeare
I am growing

I am aware
My brain and emotions
I want to share
Like a book of devotions

A life journey
My trek
A grand tourney
What the heck

My time
My ideologies
My rhyme
My mythologies

I accept it is what it is
My thoughts and impressions

I am not a brainiac or wiz
My concessions and confessions

I hope you enjoy
I hope you power through
I hope you find joy
I hope you can renew

My poems do not have punctuation or follow any grammar rules and laws. They are free to move along as they please. This poem describes my style, and I put this poem into all my books.

Punctuation

Rules and rules
English requires it
To navigate
I will not submit

My verse wants to be
Free to roam
And fall off my tongue
Not sit in a nursing home

My words are alive
Do not confine them
Let them soar
Not under your thumb

They express my life
My healings and dealings
My strife
It is not your feelings

My death is near
I know it is true
But right now who cares
Every day is brand new

Punctuation will not fence me in
Let my words explore
The known and unknown worlds
A distance shore

As I go further
I will lose my tongue
And my sight
But I will feel young

Because my mind
Will endure
What a journey
Absolutely for sure

Do not pity
The lost punctuation
Because the words dance
With flirtatious gyration

Chapter 1 - Birthdays and Holidays

These are the most exciting times of the year. Birthdays are our special days or the special day of our friends and loved ones. There is a celebration as you get older, and you realized that you have made it another year. I enjoy giving gifts and toasting one another on this unforgettable day. When I write a poem about a birthday, I want it unique, highlighting something wonderful and optimistic about the person. The message is that you are amazing, and I love you. I hope they get this message in my Birthday Poems.

Holidays are fantastic. Holidays give you the reason to be happy and to be excited about life. There are religious holidays – Christmas and Easter and national holidays of remembrance – July 4th, and Memorial Day. All these holidays give us time off from work, but more importantly, they give us free time with our families.

Time to relate, share, enjoy and participate in each other. I love holidays, and that is why I write poetry about the different days.

Birthdays

My Birthday

Birthdays are the best
Celebrating life story
You are the primary guest
Do not miss the glory

Every year adds to the splendor
You made it another year
And you did not surrender
Or give in to the fear

Life can be treacherous
There are so many pitfalls
Especially the more lecherous
The endless falls

Kids can test
And push you so hard
Make it through and your blessed
Mark it on the scorecard

Another success
Throughout a lifetime
I have played a good game of chess
But I am not longer in my prime

But life goes on
Happy Birthday to me

I am not ready to yawn
And accept a shady tree

I want zeal
I want to live
I want to feel
I want to thrive

All this is feasible
With the right attitude
My desire is appeasable
If I keep a positive mood

A mood of optimism
A mood of do ability
A mood of success
A mood of confidence

This may get tougher
Due to my health
But I will not suffer
Just expend my wealth

Spend what you must
You cannot take it with you
All in or bust
Take what is due

Enjoy each day
The best day that you can
Make it gay
Become a better man

Be cheerful
Be fearless
Not tearful
Or cheerless

Celebrate all the way
To the next birthday cake
Play your part in the play
Do not turn around or brake

Sweet Number Seven

Happy Birthday
This is your present
It is a gateway
To help you be President

You pass it to your mother
Who shares its content
Explaining one after another
What your questions meant

This book explains
How she can share
And remove the chains
To make you aware

It is her obligation
The Bible tells us so
To give you a foundation
So let us begin the show

Proverbs 22:6 Train up a child in the way he should go; even when he is old he will not depart from it.

Deuteronomy 6:5-9 Love the Lord your God with all your heart, with all your soul, and with all your strength. Take to heart these words that I give you today. Repeat them to your children. Talk about them when you're at home or away, when you lie down or get up. Write them down, and tie them around your wrist, and wear them as headbands as a reminder. Write them on the doorframes of your houses and on your gates.

Timothy 4:10-11 This is why we work hard and continue to struggle, for our hope is in the living God, who is the Savior of all people and particularly of all believers. Teach these things and insist that everyone learn them.

More people will enlist
Your church members
Vow to assist
Who else remembers

Your Sunday School leaders
Want the best for you
All these are cheerleaders
To show you what is true

You need to do your part
Read your Bible
Pray from your heart
And have no rival

There is one God
There is one way
Some find that odd
I hope they are not too late

Little Birthday Girl

Happy Birthday to you
Elizabeth my best friend
You are perfect in my view
My love will never end

I love your smart
I love your athletic
I love your pretty
I love your lively

You are sweet
You are sharing
You are understanding
You are caring

I miss you very much
I will keep you close
So we stay in touch
Anywhere I suppose

At your house
At your school
At your church
At your ballfields

But most of all
In my mind
There is a longwall
Where our memories I find

Pictures of us
Funny jokes we made
Things we did discuss
Everything we prayed

I hope you do not forget
Our precious togetherness
I am glad we met
We were so adventurous

New adventures in year eight
You are growing quick

Oh this glorious birth date
Your life is a plentiful picnic

Enjoy your life meals
Do not chew it too fast
Soak up how it feels
Make every moment last

Today is your day
Happy Birthday
It is your day
Forevermore the best day

Birthday Again

I have another birthday
One more year
Let us downplay
And save the cheer

I have had many good ones
I plan to have many more
I have eaten cake in tons
I have blown out candles galore

What is one more celebration
We all celebrate them
Like the stars in the constellation
Routine and another ho hum

But what if I say
I am kidding
I want the display
I am admitting

Display the cake
Display the cards
Display the presents
Display the smiles

Five or Fifty
I want the recognition
Cool and nifty
Bring on the magician and musician

I am happy everyone remembered
This special ceremonial occasion
Another numbered and rendered
Extending my life equation

I am delighted my loves are here
Kissing and hugging me
And I want to hear
Happy Birthday was sung with glee

College Dorm Birthdays

I went to college not knowing a soul
Smith Hall was my home
And no one was in control
Like days of the hippodrome

Wild foot races
Heavy drinking
Behavior disgraces
What were we thinking

On our own
We had the excuses
If we had known
All the lumps and bruises

Through this merriment
Friends are made
A grand experiment
Our friendships did not fade

We celebrated this time
Especially our birthdays
We were in our prime
Our journeys would not delay

We had different majors
From different towns
But we were teenagers
Enjoying the sights and sounds

Out birthday celebrations
Always held at little bar and grill
Close to our dormitory locations
Not dampening our will

For three years
We celebrated our births
By raising beers
For all its worth

We enjoyed each other
Celebrating this season
As a true brother
And it was for this reason

I have these fond thoughts
We were close
Living out the plots
Of our own very own show

To Jeff
To Tom
To Richard
To Ricardo

And all the other attendees
Who existed and attended
Enjoying our birthdays with ease
I hope your birthdays are splendid

Holidays

Memorial Day

Honor that serviceman
Remember his sacrifice
A time to be born again
For all who paid the price

This a solemn occasion
To respect these men
Who was part of many invasions
Defending on country time again

Visit the cemetery
And place a flag
A little scary
Do not get gagged

I get choked up
Thinking of my kinfolk
Ever since I was a pup
This was no joke

There is a crush of emotions
Recalling their blood sweat and tears
But many go through the motions
Enjoying the holiday with their peers

Memorial Day is the start of the summer holidays
Barbeques and swimming pools
Enjoy these longer days
And the end of attending schools

Respect this dual nature yearly
Memorial and jubilee
A significant event most clearly
Remembering why we are free

Easter

A celebration of gratitude
Celebrating Jesus has risen
An event of proportionate magnitude
Releasing us from prison

A prison of sin
Separated from His Most High
Jesus did ultimately win
After being tortured and crucified

We were and are set free
If we turn and repent

Accept Jesus as Lord
And God raised him from dead

How wonderful a day
God took on our pain
We can pray
To remove the stain

We pay tribute to Jesus the King
Praising his sacrifice
Singing and worshipping
Thinking of God and paradise

Some attend local congregations
Dressing in new clothes
Usually with our closest relations
Followed by food and touching elbows

From here it diverges
Depending upon tradition
And what the moment urges
And everyone and their ambition

Some hang with the flock
Some take a short nap
Some take a walk
Some want to just yak

What is monumental and decisive
We recognize our new beginning
And it can be unpopular and divisive
It requires our committing

Committing to a new life
A life to change our ways
End all our strife
On this righteous holiday

Halloween

A holiday to not take seriously
Enjoy the costumes and games
Nothing mysterious
Contrary to all the claims

I dressed as a pirate
And a janitor
There were no riots
A happy atmosphere

We collected candy
Neighborhood to neighborhood
Out as long as we fancy
I had an extraordinary boyhood

As I grew older
The Halloween tricks
Became much bolder
We were out for our kicks

No treat prank their house
No treat then chalk house
No treat then roll their house
No treat then egg their house

This did not last long
Girls and dances
Let us go along
And make advances

This went on for several years
A dating and mating routine
We were happy with lots of cheer
Great to enjoy Halloween

I remember laughter
I remember excitement
I remember comedy
I remember merriment

A joyous occasion
If you go with the flow
The kid invasion
Now a grand show

And so it goes
In old my old age
Lurking in the shadows
My kids turn the page

My kids and family friends
Dress and enjoy the holiday
The fun transcends
To the end of my days

Valentines for Me

Here we are
A day of love
Not a love czar
But a romantic dove

A dove of peace
A dove of understanding
A dove of increase
A dove of expanding

Increasing kindness
Expanding commitment
Restricting blindness
Eliminating resentment

Love is ever increasing
Building up over time
Endorphins releasing
Happiness on the climb

Climbing to a new place
Climbing to a new high
Climbing to a new grace
Climbing to a new cry

A cry of passion
A cry of affection
A cry to cash in
On a unique inflection

Refuting egotism
Ignoring offenses
Abandoning schism
Lowering our defenses

Growing appreciation
Growing generosity
Growing dedication
Growing reciprocity

Always climbing higher
Striving to soar
A willing sojourner and flier

To love intensely and enjoy

My Patriot Song

Happy Birthday
To our great nation
It takes my breath away
Both resolute and duration

As a republic for the masses
We have tried to represent
Without stations and classes
The founders intent

A grand gamble
To make people free
A strong preamble
For the world to see

We were the first
Many have followed
An unquenchable thirst
But it can be hard to swallow

There are outrages
Staring us in the face
From our history pages
What a disgrace

Keeping people in chains
A terrible slight
Killing the Indians on the plains
A horrendous blight

Holding women back
Not allowing them rights
Abortion kills millions of blacks
And millions of whites

But is this all
There is to the United States
To miss our call
And what separates

Separates us from oppression
One person with absolute rule
Fascism and communism aggression
And others of the tyrant pool

Our ability to change and flex

And to remember distinctly
Through our constitutional checks
Stating a truth succinctly

We are in control
The people can altar
Through the voting poll
When our leaders falter

Voting is the right
That keeps us strong
So we must fight
To carry this tradition along

Traditions of our glorious past
Maybe with a few flaws
But we need to hold steadfast
To our great cause

To make people unbound
From whatever oppresses
Let us articulate and astound
What our history expresses

We lead the world
In reducing oppression
Our flag is unfurled
To fight these transgressions

Transgressions of injustice
Transgressions of poverty

Transgressions of race
Transgressions of hate

We push to correct wrongs
Not always timely and correct
But sing our proud songs
And fix what is not perfect

Stand upright and proud
Fly our flag high
Sing our praises out loud
We are not the bad guy

But democratic patriots
Believing in individual liberties
Spreading a brilliant radiance
And the endless possibilities

Possibilities of prosperity
Throughout the earth
Seeking a shared destiny
For everyone from birth

Democracy is not a dream
Freedoms advance
With our grand theme
Join in the dance

Celebrate our championships
Proclaim our glories
Cherish our relationships
And tell our remarkable story

Christmas

A day of memories and dreams
A day of surprises and delights
A day of visions and memes
A day of encounters and highlights

Christmas means so many things
From gifts to charity
From paupers to kings
From rarity to regularity

The birth of Jesus is rarity
The commercialism of gifts is plurality
To many Christ is clarity
And others buy and spend is normality

Christ is the one true God

And gifts are the worlds gods
Along with sexual deviance and fraud
And penny pinchers and tightwads

Why oh why can we not see
We have missed the truth
We are chained instead of free
We took these gods to the voting booth

And their gods prevailed
They won the election
Their agenda is veiled
And their actions a deflection

A deflection from their real plan
To make all living creatures the same
With one world god who will be man
Man will be the entire con game

New man will not believe that God exists
With morals and morality
Who is and what and persists
Giving us immortality

New man will believe he is right
He has knowledge and pride
He is the light and bright
He will not be denied

Denied his strength
Denied his intelligence
Denied his worldview

Denied his divinity

But new man is not living
New man is not growing
New man is not giving
New man is not forgiving

There is an illusion
There is a fantasy
There is a delusion
There is agony

New man wants your burdens eased
New man wants you to be fooled
New man wants you to be pleased
New man wants you to be ruled

New man wants to control your health
New man wants to control your news
New man wants to control your wealth
New man wants to control your lives

New man wants to control your mind
Telling you right from wrong
Making you deaf and blind
Hoping you play along

Play along to the lies
Abortion is not murder
There is no Christianity
Everyone is the same

But we are not one
We have names
Can this travesty be undone
Or will it end in flames

How can we stop it
What would Christ do
He gave us a writ
It is not new

Share the gospels
Tell all far and wide
Believe the apostles
Jesus died

But he is alive
Dying for our sins
Allowing us to strive
Along with His wins

This is Christmas day
Jesus is born
We celebrate and pray
And be warned and mourn

Warned man is forgetful
Warned man is selfish
Warned man is irresponsible
Warned man is dangerous

Mourn those who do not believe
Mourn those who believe but do not share

Mourn those who twist and deceive
Mourn those caught in the devils snare

Remember your duty
To share Gods story
And His remarkable beauty
And His infinite glory

Chapter 2 - Politics and Issues of 2020

The past election was one of the ugliest on record. There is no doubt the country is divided with so many people hating one another. I witnessed name-calling, illogical arguments, false arguments (lying), and false dilemma arguments. Friends against friends and family against family. A very disgusting exhibition of civility.

Today, I listen to the news one year after the election, and one-sided is entirely different from what they said they would do if elected to the Presidency. I think many were duped into believing what they wanted to hear. They wanted to get rid of a rude, obnoxious, grass President and they did get rid of him. They did not use common sense to appreciate and evaluate who they were elected to the Presidency and the consequences of that result, but that is not new in the history of the United States.

There is a winner and a loser in every election. You can claim fraud but too bad. If you thought there was going to be fraud, then it must be addressed before the election. If you wait until after the election, then it is too late. Many do not have the guts to stand up and fight injustice after the fact.

This chapter addresses issues that I think are unjust. My most significant hot button issue is abortion. I will never understand how so many people can support murdering millions and millions of babies. In the United States, it is close to 60 million since the 1970s, and in the world, there are 60 million abortions annually. How terrifying. As a Christian, this one issue devastates my soul. I find it even more abhorring that Christians support abortion.

You may not agree with my thoughts or poems, but that is life. I hope you can understand my point of view.

Election

What a shocker
So many casts votes
Sitting in a rocker
Captains of both boats

What a gigantic gap
The two parties represent
It is hard to unwrap
Their central positions and content

My candidate is loud and grass
The challenger slow and insider
They want to get a pass
And be a spoiler and divider

Divide our common needs
Spoil our communal peace
Grow a bunch of weeds
And it must cease

What is worthwhile
What is bane
What is vile
What is insane

Both political parties
Demonize one another
Creating two armies
Brother against brother

One wants more and more
Taking care of everyone
An open free store
Which is looted and overrun

Overrun with global welfare
Overrun with irresponsibility
Overrun with many things unfair
Overrun with hostility

I saw the daily riots

I saw the craziness
Democrats approving silence
A world of haziness

Do they care
Do they see the unease
Do they live the nightmare
Do they understand the disease

Selfishness
Injustice
Mayhem
Anarchy

Half of Americans want harmony
Half of Americans want security
Half of Americans want to live cheerfully
Half of Americans want obscurity

Our candidate is loud
And bluntly offensive
He is a patriot and proud
His manner very intensive

He lost the election
Earning 72 million voters
Building a connection
Making us feel like owners

Owners of our actions
Owners of our cities
Owners of our states

Owners of our countries

It is our precious lives
It is our hard earned money
It is our earnestness and drives
It is our milk and honey

But not today
And not tomorrow
What we want fades away
We are in a freak show

Give everyone everything
Let them sit around
And be their own king
King with a crown

A crown of authority
A crown of dignity
A crown of superiority
A crown of benignity

But this is not true
What can you get for free
You did not earn the view
But you enjoy the spree

Spree to riot
Spree to loot
Spree to kill
Spree to hate

Every vote cast
For hate and disorder
Maybe someone will ask
Do you want a one world order

One climate peace accord
One global trade deal
One world everyone can afford
One socialist communist ideal

Socialism has failed
Everywhere it has tried
Many ruined lives unveiled
Communism a poor guide

Share your wealth
Share your heritage
Share your health
Share your America

But why
Why ruin the cookbook
That made the American Pie
The world looks to as a nook

A safe place
A place to succeed
Not a superior race
A place to exceed

Try hard
Read

Study
Work

Make a life
A life that is yours
With no strife
For all your years

One you have earned
You have made for yourself
It cannot be overturned
So take pride in oneself

Pride of family
Pride of accomplishment
Pride of success
Pride of eternalness

A free country
You helped to create
Many branches in the tree
Mighty and forever great

Feel

What does a baby feel
In the womb or newborn
Joy and pain are real
The debate is torn

Torn between alive or what
A newborn is alive
There is no but
It can live and strive

What about a fetus
In the womb
Do you have a treatise
Or do you leave the room

No regard for science
It is living
Against your defiance
Answers are missing

When does the heartbeat
Not months but weeks
Six weeks like a drumbeat
The heart speaks

When the heart stops
We are declared dead
The blood flow drops
And life has fled

If you are born
You are alive with heartbeats
But not if you are unborn
Who cares if it repeats

Then comes your nervous process
Developing soon after the heart starts
Reflexes begin to progress
And pain is its counterpart

Yes pain is present
In the womb
Many will dissent
But it is not your gloom or doom

Babies move away from the intruder
Babies shrink from the abortions tools

Babies jerk from the pursuer
Babies not understanding the rules

How about brain waves
The fetus starts around forty days
We are on our way to our graves
If our brains are not ablaze

What is life
A heartbeat
A nervous system
A brain wave

I want all three
Many will disagree
But they are free
To argue with me

Global Warming

Is it true
Or is it false
Is it a coup
Or a waltz

A dance of rising tides
A dance of dying animals
A dance of violent storms
A dance of human extinction

A dance of global pain
A dance of damnation
A dance of blame
A dance of elimination

A dance to control
A dance of dominance
A dance to bankroll
A dance of prominence

Global warming is a reality
It is something unusual
And we will agree
It is extremely cruel

But can a man stop it
Can a man end the conflict
Can man recommit
To stop being an addict

An addict to coal and wood
An addict to our cars
An addict to beef and food
An addict to Santa Cause

Buy more gifts and things
Do I need them or not
We are all gods and kings
Demanding ours on the spot

We are a large group
A grand number
A marching troop
Unwilling to encumber

Do not hold back my wants
Wants of unnecessary excess
Go to my shops and restaurants
And my right to progress

Live a happy life
Playing with my toys

Creating invisible strife
Global warming noise

Who will sacrifice
Just give it away
And leave paradise
Push away from the buffet

Those with the most
Cut their fossil fuel careers
Tax them coast to coast
Increase their tears and fears

Close all their doors
Shut out of the American dream
Now they are a whores
Their lives changed to extremes

When Do You Live

I do not know
When you live
You must tiptoe
The issue to survive

Survive abuse
Survive intolerance
Survive hatred
Survive injustice

Kill a baby
Whenever you want
Alive maybe
All so nonchalant

Women rights are first
No exceptions
What can be worse
Than ignorant misconceptions

When does life begin
Christians believe at conception
Science has many spins
And fixed perceptions

Is life when DNA completes at three days
Is life when the heart beats at 24 days
Is life when brain waves are recorded at 43 days
Is life when a baby can live outside the womb at 140 days

Or is life when a woman decides
I can abort my unique child
And the world ultimately divides
The world goes crazy wild

One side says control my life
Damn human life
One side says save every life
Precious human life

Who is responsible for human health
Is it each 3.8 billion women on the globe
Or is it the elected commonwealth
Or some unelected justice in a black robe

Every human being is responsible for these losses
You cannot hide behind a lack of knowledge
You cannot hide behind your crosses
You must reasonably acknowledge

At 20 weeks it can live outside the womb
Start here and make the laws the same
Bring everyone who cares in the room
And quit the shame and blame game

Persecution

Persecution is hostility
Persecution is ill treatment
Persecution is unfair treatment
Persecution is an abusive treatment

Any act of ill will
Can be persecution
Sometimes a bitter pill
No real solution

Majority or minority
Whatever color
No authority or absolute authority
Few dollars or a bunch of dollars

Atheism or Christian
Does not matter
This is not fiction
Never ending chapter

People will hate
People will control
People will attack
People will kill

This is our story
Story of humanity
Journey of fury
And depravity

Christians are oppressed
In many ways
This is not a test
For it happens nowadays

Christians are called names
Christians are beaten
Christians are rejected
Christians are murdered

I live in the USA
Things are not like that here
Maybe not today
But listen and rehear

Bad News
2 Timothy 3:12 (ESV) [12] Indeed, all who desire to live a godly life in Christ Jesus will be persecuted,
1 John 3:13 (ESV) [13] Do not be surprised, brothers,[a] that the world hates you.

Good News
1 Peter 3:14 (ESV) [14] But even if you should suffer for righteousness' sake, you will be blessed. Have no fear of them, nor be troubled,
Matthew 5:10 (ESV) [10] "Blessed are those who are persecuted for righteousness' sake, for theirs is the kingdom of heaven.

But not in my United States
Not in my USA city
Not with my friends and mates

Not in my church committee

We are called by Christ
To be one body
Not cut and sliced
And not inferior or shoddy

One body as a whole
Caring for one another
Where I take a stroll
Or miles from my sister and brother

A Christian persecuted in Louisiana
A Christian persecuted in St Louis
A Christian persecuted in Facebook
A Christian persecuted in the World

All the same to our Lord
And it should be the same for us
We are on the same game board
Some castled in blissful snugness

Snugness from the action
Snugness from the abuses
Snugness from murderous fractions
Snugness from the bruises

The Bible is clear
We are part of the One
So shed a heartfelt tear
For our Savior the Son

Do not end now
Do not forget
Do not isolate
Do not think your set

Jesus wants us to love
He wants us to get along
Not be under the thumb of
Those strong and wrong

Many are harmed
Not just us Christian Saints
Remember the abused
And their complaints

Black lives of import
And they have a point
Not useless chatter
An ugly wart

Muslims matter too
China restricts their birth pace
This is more than a few
Millions lost without a trace

Women are left behind
Why does their paycheck lag
And the world is blind
Do you have to nag

Nagged to get your issues addressed
Nagged to listen and learn

Nagged to help and invest
Nagged to make it your turn

It is our turn to be accountable
To use our capabilities
To be countable
To end these hostilities

Christians have a call
To address conflicts
No matter how small
And no quick fix

God wants us to help
God wants us to intervene
God wants us to have compassion
God wants us to act

Act in many ways
Donate your time
Donate your money
Donate your prayers

God wants you to know
God loves everyone
Christians must acknowledge
We are under the same sun

Scriptures for One Body

Romans 12:4 (ESV) [4] For as in one body we have many members,[a] and the members do not all have the same function,

1 Corinthians 10:17 (ESV) [17] Because there is one bread, we who are many are one body, for we all partake of the one bread.

1 Corinthians 12:12 (ESV) One Body with Many Members [12] For just as the body is one and has many members, and all the members of the body, though many, are one body, so it is with Christ.
1 Corinthians 12:13 (ESV) [13] For in one Spirit we were all baptized into one body—Jews or Greeks, slaves[a] or free—and all were made to drink of one Spirit.
1 Corinthians 12:14 (ESV) [14] For the body does not consist of one member but of many.
Ephesians 2:16 (ESV) [16] and might reconcile us both to God in one body through the
Cross, thereby killing the hostility

Children Of Men

Who is this man
Mortals of man
Mankind of man
People of man

Who is he
Who is she
Who is thee
Who is me

But children
Made in Gods image
And we are many million
In life scrimmage

People of color
People of race
People of religion
People of haste

Haste to blame one another
Haste to accuse one another
Haste to hate one another
Haste to destroy one another

Do we understand
Do we care
Do we walk hand in hand
Do we stand there

Stand there in dogma
Stand there in fairness
Stand there in belief
Stand there in bareness

Naked to face God
To seek His forgiveness
Knowing I am flawed
My sin of impulsiveness

Rushing about
Wanting it all
Waiting for a give out
Not waiting for the call

The call to accept
There is more to living
But I just slept
Instead of forgiving

Forgiving my self
Forgiving my family
Forgiving my friends
Forgiving my humanity

Is it too late
To be embraced
To enter the gate
And to taste

Taste the love
Taste the goodness

Taste the mercy
Taste the assurance

No it has not past
The final chance
So be quite fast
To enter the dance

Dance with Jesus
Dance with God
Dance with the Holy Spirit
Dance with Christs bride

The Bride of Christ
Gather in Christ
Body of Christ
The church is Christ

The church is your family
The church is your base
The church is no anomaly
The church is your place

Grow in the church
Disciple in the church
Serve in the church
Reconcile in the church

Not always pretty
Not always nice
What a pity
Take my advice

Better there
Then anywhere
A house of prayer
Jesus is near

Near to our hearts
Near to our thoughts
Near to our hurts
Near to our faults

Accept His presence
Accept His gift
Accept His peace
Accept His love

Notes

Proverbs 8:4 New International Version (NIV)
4 "To you, O people, I call out;
I raise my voice to all **mankind**.

Proverbs 8:31 New International Version (NIV)
31 rejoicing in his whole world
and delighting in **mankind.**

Proverbs 15:11 New International Version (NIV)
11 Death and Destruction[a] lie open before the Lord—
how much more do **human** hearts!

Psalm 11:4 New International Version (NIV)

⁴ The Lord is in his holy temple;
the Lord is on his heavenly throne.
He observes everyone on earth;
his eyes examine **them**.

Psalm 12:8 New International Version (NIV)
⁸ who freely strut about
when what is vile is honored by the **human race**.

Psalm 14:2 New International Version (NIV)
² The Lord looks down from heaven
on all **mankind**
to see if there are any who understand,
any who seek God.

Psalm 21:10 New International Version (NIV)
¹⁰ You will destroy their descendants from the earth,
their posterity from **mankind.**

Psalm 33:13 New International Version (NIV)
¹³ From heaven the Lord looks down
and sees all **mankind**;

Psalm 53:2 New International Version (NIV)
² God looks down from heaven
on all **mankind**
to see if there are any who understand,
any who seek God.

Psalm 57:4 New International Version (NIV)
⁴ I am in the midst of lions;
I am forced to dwell among ravenous beasts—

men whose teeth are spears and arrows,
whose tongues are sharp swords.

Psalm 58[a]
For the director of music. To the tune of "Do Not Destroy." Of David. A *miktam*.[b]
¹ Do you rulers indeed speak justly?
Do you judge **people** with equity?

Psalm 66:5 New International Version (NIV)
⁵ Come and see what God has done,
his awesome deeds for **mankind**!

Psalm 89:47 New International Version (NIV)
⁴⁷ Remember how fleeting is my life.
For what futility you have created all **humanity**!

Psalm 90:3 New International Version (NIV)
³ You turn **people** back to dust,
saying, "Return to dust, you mortals."

Psalm 107:8 (4 times in Psalm 107) New International Version (NIV)
⁸ Let them give thanks to the Lord for his unfailing love
and his wonderful deeds for **mankind**,

Psalm 115:16 New International Version (NIV)
¹⁶ The highest heavens belong to the Lord,
but the earth he has given to **mankind**.

Psalm 145:12 New International Version (NIV)
¹² so that all **people** may know of your mighty acts

and the glorious splendor of your kingdom.

Ecclesiastes 1:13 New International Version (NIV)
13 I applied my mind to study and to explore by wisdom all that is done under the heavens. What a heavy burden God has laid on **mankind**!

Ecclesiastes 2:3 New International Version (NIV)
3 I tried cheering myself with wine, and embracing folly—my mind still guiding me with wisdom. I wanted to see what was good for **people** to do under the heavens during the few days of their lives.

Ecclesiastes 3:10 New International Version (NIV)
10 I have seen the burden God has laid on the **human race**.

Ecclesiastes 3:18 New International Version (NIV)
18 I also said to myself, "As for **humans,** God tests them so that they may see that they are like the animals.

Ecclesiastes 3:19 New International Version (NIV)
19 Surely the fate of **human beings** is like that of the animals; the same fate awaits them both: As one dies, so dies the other. All have the same breath[a]; humans have no advantage over animals. Everything is meaningless.

Ecclesiastes 8:11 New International Version (NIV)
11 When the sentence for a crime is not quickly carried out, **people**'s hearts are filled with schemes to do wrong.

Ecclesiastes 9:3 New International Version (NIV)

³ This is the evil in everything that happens under the sun: The same destiny overtakes all. The hearts of **people**, moreover, are full of evil and there is madness in their hearts while they live, and afterward they join the dead.

Ecclesiastes 9:12 New International Version (NIV)
¹² Moreover, no one knows when their hour will come:
As fish are caught in a cruel net,
or birds are taken in a snare,
so **people** are trapped by evil times
that fall unexpectedly upon them.

Jeremiah 32:19 New International Version (NIV)
¹⁹ great are your purposes and mighty are your deeds. Your eyes are open to the ways of all **mankind**; you reward each person according to their conduct and as their deeds deserve.

Ezekiel 31:14 New International Version (NIV)
¹⁴ Therefore no other trees by the waters are ever to tower proudly on high, lifting their tops above the thick foliage. No other trees so well-watered are ever to reach such a height; they are all destined for death, for the earth below, among **mortals** who go down to the realm of the dead.

Daniel 2:38 New International Version (NIV)
³⁸ in your hands he has placed all **mankind** and the beasts of the field and the birds in the sky. Wherever they live, he has made you ruler over them all. You are that head of gold.

Daniel 10:16 New International Version (NIV)
¹⁶ Then one who looked like a **man**[a] touched my lips, and I opened my mouth and began to speak. I said to the one standing before me, "I am overcome with anguish because of the vision, my lord, and I feel very weak.

Joel 1:12 New International Version (NIV)
¹² The vine is dried up
and the fig tree is withered;
the pomegranate, the palm and the apple[a] tree—
all the trees of the field—are dried up.
Surely the **people**'s joy
is withered away.

Micah 5:7 New International Version (NIV)
⁷ The remnant of Jacob will be
in the midst of many **peoples**
like dew from the Lord,
like showers on the grass,
which do not wait for anyone
or depend on man.

Mark 3:28 New International Version (NIV)
28 Truly I tell you, people can be forgiven all their sins and every slander they utter,

Election Debate

The election debate
Was troublesome and frank
No one talked straight
Belonging in the septic tank

Their arguments stunk
Full of crap
Were they drunk
Or caught in a trap

They hated Trump
No matter what
He was a chump
And a horses butt

They would do anything
To vote him out
Dispose of the bully king
With a knockout

But his policies were sound
They fueled a recovery
Our country to rebound
Not a new discovery

A strong national defense
Lower taxes to promote economic growth
Keep illegal immigrants out with a border fence
And decisions to protect our autonomy

Do not make us
Accountable to world organizations
With their global smugness
And the endless frustrations

We will pay the price
Through unfair trade
Ending our paradise
Our greatness will fade

He supported the police
Wanting everyone to be secure
And the police to keep the peace
Not creating any detours

Detours to more crimes
By defunding the police
It reminds you of the end times
When civility will cease

But is it the end
Start of the apocalypse
Too late to amend
We need to come to grips

This is part of history
The ebb and flow
A grand mystery
It allows the country to grow

Why people vote sporadically
Changing their minds

Sometimes radically
With the blowing of the winds

But all I know
This all will pass
As it did long ago
Just handle it with class

No profanity
No bullying
No cursing
No bruising

Use your speech
Let everyone talk
Ideas debated each
Even if there is a deadlock

The mood will change
People will change
Votes will change
Leaders will change

But do not change our character
Our free elections
Our liberties and freedoms
Our equalities

Improve upon these
There will be mistakes
And missed keys
Heartaches and headaches

So stand tall
Salute the flag
The country will not fall
If we do not treat the flag as a rag

The flag has a prominence
A national representation
Reflecting our dominance
As a democratic nation

Fighting for democracies
Throughout the world
And our democratic qualities
So keep our flag unfurled

Immigration

There is illegal immigration
Swarms and swarms of foreigners
Overrunning our nation
Why do we let them cut corners

They can follow the rules
Made by our lawmakers
They are fools
And horrible fakers

If these people are in need
Escaping persecution
Wanting to be freed
And seeking a solution

Then change our laws
Giving them a way
A grand pause
To this senseless fray

Set up welcoming camps
Where they can be vetted
Escaping their tormentors
And not indebted

Indebted to drug cartels
Or horrible villains
Adding to our prison cells
And spending billions

Inspect their health
A crash course in the United States
Teaching them English
And know if they have a trade

Give them time to assimilate
To our way of living
Give them a fate
And a bountiful thanksgiving

Transport those with qualifications
To the places in need of a workforce
If they have job limitations
Then add them to a course

To evaluate their potential

Teach them a skill
To meet our employment needs
Where everyone moves ahead

Give them a license
Give them a social security number
Give them voter registration
Give them medical insurance

Change our national identity
Nothing will be given free
But we will give them dignity
So let us agree

There is a better process
To make us all stakeholders
Why all the fess
Our nation has broad shoulders

Taxes

Who wants to pay more taxes
Why do you vote for a President
Who wants more money
Who wants to expand the tent

Give away tax dollars
To those in need
We called them ballers
Hustlers with greed

There are those in need
Do not get me wrong
A safety net to feed
It makes our country strong

But a cellphone is not an essential
And food stamps to waste and spree
We gloss over their potential
And they are not free

They are dependent
Upon the United States
Not independent
Missing their fates

What is more cruel
To remove ambition
And just a bumbling fool
No success or fruition

Change the paradigm
Make a new reality
Give them a way to climb
To what they can be

Make life changing programs
Push training and relocation
Break the bureaucratic log jams
There is one more causation

Change the education inefficiency
Push understanding and learning
Teaching subjects to reduce their deficiency
Stop our nation from burning

This is a pandemic
Reverse the educational triangle
Everyone does not deserve the nonacademic
These are rewards to dangle

Only students who pass reading and math
Move to the unique schools
They get band and athletics on this path
Make these policies the rules

A great upheaval
A bloodbath for the education enterprise
Is this horrible and evil
Or must the system capsize

To prepare our country to compete
We must change how we think
A gigantic bureaucracy to defeat
We must not blink

Change how we educate
Change how we train
Change how we relocate
Change how we reward

Reward those who strive
Strive to succeed
Who have a drive
And have agreed

Agreed to move
Agreed to groom
Agreed to learn
Agreed to work

Reward them with our taxes
Pay them a wage
Cover all their finances
Turn the page

A new mission
A new life story
A new vision
A new glory

Revamp how we teach our kids
Revamp how we spend our money
Revamp how we retrain workers
Revamp how we see the nation

A nation that cares
A nation that thrives
A nation that shares
A nation to change lives

Taxation is fair
If we change the nation
A burden to bear
To improve our foundation

Woke Culture

Craziness
Make everyone shamed
Intellectual laziness
These false claims

This country has made great strides

To address our racial past
These policies require all to take sides
Creating a new caste

We are exempt
Because we were slaves
I see an attempt
To hide the storm waves

Crime sprees
Blatant deception
A growing disease
Is my perception

Justify the mayhem
Give it a spin
Motivate them
To commit their sins

More robberies
More beatings
More rapes
More murders

Promote defund the police
Make this the woke banner
Ruin our tranquility and peace
Crime is a personal manner

What is the end game
To create such a state
A reparation frame

At a future date

Bombard the population
Making them feel guilty
Solve the guilt with reparations
This is silly

You cannot change the past
All you can do is understand it
Seek solutions for the downcast
Our politicians need to use their wit

Create training centers
Create all expenses paid
Create relocation packages
Create a new way

A way forward and ahead
To make this country healthier
Stop all crime and bloodshed
And make everyone wealthier

The past is gone
We have today
An unprecedented dawn
To end this senseless fray

All Lives Matter

All lives matter
Racism is to segregate
What hateful chatter
Easy to debate

Our laws are clear
Cannot discriminate by color
A complete smear
Ask a scholar

We go back
Back to hard times
Segregation of all who were black
These were horrific crimes

Martin Luther King marched

Marching for laws that were equal
The old system was parched
We were ready for a sequel

A sequel to our history
Where all are liberated
A baffling mystery
This liberty is devastated

Make people slaves again
To the color of their skin
Lose their hard earned gains
No one will win

Spur unrest
Create a special class
Their problems not addressed
No one will get a pass

More crimes
More radicalism
More anarchy
More violence

Everyone will suffer
Because of this story
Society will create a buffer
A safe territory

The poor will lose jobs
The poor will lose shops
The poor will lose housing

The poor will lose family

Their plight will not be made better
Through unnecessary conflict
They will be debtors
To a belief that is imperfect

Chapter 3 - What Makes Me Tick

How do you know what makes you tick? When do you know what makes you tick? I do not know when I became self-aware. I do know that I never knew what caused me to tick until I was in my fifties. I seemed to slow down long enough to listen to myself. I think that I became self-aware when I became a Stephen Minister.

A Stephen Minister is a layperson who talks to people who are having issues. You try to be empathic, you need to be a good listen, and you ask open questions. I think I began to think of other people and their feelings, making me feel my feelings more and more.

These poems are scraps of my thoughts about myself. I know the Bible has a gigantic influence on my life. I may not be the most righteous person, but I know I love Jesus and God. I am aware that for most of my life, I chased money and success. I made this my scorecard. I thought if I had a million dollars in cash at one point in my life, I would be wealthy. How foolish.

I have always been driven by checklists, goals, visions, and missions. I planned and executed based upon these priorities. Did this hide worry and stress in my life? Maybe or probably it did cause my issues, but I hid it so well. Not until my fifties was I overwhelmed by anxiety or the disassociation of cognitive and emotional thought patterns.

I still have problems. They can be activated or aggravated by stress, arguments, fights, disagreements, and misunderstandings. Amitriptyline has helped tremendously, but there are side effects. No reading and writing with this medicine. The drug slows me down. I am not asking Amitriptyline, and it has enabled me to write poetry, organize this book, and publish this book. My symptoms are creeping back, and I will take medicine if my issues get worse.

I have written poems about my medical adventure, and my first book of poetry, Uplifting Poems About the Death of a Loved One, was all about his journey.

Do not be too critical of my ticks. We all have them, and everyone needs a little grace.

Bible

Gods message to us
To help us grow
Smart and strong
It is the truth

So many stories
To give us help
Along our way
At any age

All stories point
To one man

Jesus Christ
Our Lord and Savior

He is God
He died for us
He paid for our sins
He rose from the dead

He promises us
If we believe he is Lord
And God raised him from the dead
We will be saved from our sins

We will go to heaven
We will see God, Jesus and Holy Spirit
We will see all the heroes of the Bible
We will see our families

That is a promise
That I believe
That many do believe
That is the truth

My hope is you
Will someday believe
What the Bible says
And promises

Disappointed

Really
Why should you be disappointed
Involuntarily
Fault cannot be pinpointed

She misunderstood
She disagreed
She thought you no good
She never guaranteed

You were pushy
You were needy
You were never cushy
Maybe you were seedy

But does it really matter
Her fault or your fault
The earth did not shatter
Or neither struck by a thunderbolt

No matter how hard
You all surely tried
Relationships have no safeguards
Or commitments implied

Two people going through life
One day at the time
Dodging and avoiding the strife
Only wishing your lives will rhyme

Please God just one other person
Somewhere on earth
Things cannot worsen
Surely God defines my worth

He is the foundation
We have built our lives
Indeed there is not damnation
Our world thrives

There are kids and parents
Work and social events
Now and then a few declarants
And Christmas and birthday presents

Life goes on
With Jesus on your arm
Forget days foregone
And do not rush to the funny farm

Because life proceeds
Do not think you are alone
Jesus graciously leads
He will not disown

He may seem far away
But He is right there
This is not a cliche
It is all about prayer

Pray relentlessly
Beg for His support

Not helplessly
You all have a passport

A one way ticket to the promised land
Because you have believed
How is this not grand
You have not been deceived

Heaven awaits
Holy Spirit is here too
Loneliness He hates
But this is true

Believe in your heart
Jesus is Lord
Your life will never fall apart
And you will never be ignored

And add that God raised Him
From the grave
It is a glorious hymn
You are no longer a slave

Share this Gospel message
And you will have friends
Abandon the wreckage
And reap God's dividends

Checklist

I have had one forever
Once it is on the list
A grand endeavor
Not to be missed

Get it done
Can be transposable
Not always fun
Quick as possible

Which one first
Which one second
Which one makes a difference
Which one is important

From A1 to C1
A ranking tactic
Works in the long run
Way too didactic

How did I get consumed
By this need to check it off
Too much to do I assumed
Me and my mighty trough

A trough of obsession
A trough of greed
A trough of pride

A trough of ambition

But where am I now
Chasing a disorder
Nothing but a sow
Who is out of order

I must throw the list away
It does not matter to me
Who cares if I stray
And become carefree

I have been told
Does it matter
In the past it was gold
Today dung splatter

I have changed
To get relief
Not to be deranged
But to reduce my grief

Go away systematic rules
To accomplish tasks
These are just tools
Anxiety and depression masks

Masks of fatigue
Masks of rages
Masks of technique
Masks of past ages

Take mine down
Get rid of it
I want to stay around
And keep my wit

My Dance

I did not respect my health
Keep track of my friends
Sharpen and expand my mind
Or appreciating my wealth

Do I have remorse
Concerning all these thoughts
A strange force
Bothering me a lot

Why do they bother me now
I have lived a long time
Will it change somehow
My story rhyme

The pace my life progresses
In a repetitive motion
Failures and successes
Indifferences and emotions

Up and down
Round and round
A priest or a clown
Mute or with sound

What I have learned
Is I can fight it
But I will get burned
Or use my wit

Learn the dance
Forward and back
Retreat and advance
Seek peace and attack

Dancing is easy
Moving to the beat
Not at all cheesy
Beautiful when expressed

The dance presents understanding
And maturity
Your emotional health is expanding
Giving you security

Security to be yourself
Security to let someone go
Security to be alone
Security to be alright

Alright is not hard
Or overrated
You can lower your guard
Throw away things hated

Why walk on eggshells
Every step of the way
Jump at each bell
To keep the family gay

Wait to be invited

Like a waiting taxicab
Feel judged and indicted
A jab or a stab

Sounds very frightening
But all I wish
Is emotional enlightening
And to dance with a swish

Twirl about
Skip to the tune
These things have no clout
I am immune

I dance with charming traits
Knowing I am good

And so much awaits
Without any falsehoods

Taken for granted
Highlighting my faults
Their beliefs are slanted
But I will waltz

To their reverberations
And their misrepresentations
Dancing on my foundations
Forgetting the frustrations

My dance is divine
To and foe
And it is all mine
The ebb and flow

The coming and going
Enjoying the song
That rhythm flowing
I have grown strong

Remember

I remember
When I was younger
I was a member
And did not hunger

I was strong
I was healthy and fit
I sang a happy song
I had my wit

I did not worry
For my health
I was in a hurry
To make my wealth

This was my affiliation
Make money and win
Part of a capitalistic nation
But this was a sin

To chase money
Forgetting the rest
It was not sunny
Much distress

I wanted it all
But pursuing wealth
Created a great brawl
Lurking with stealth

Destroyed relations
Forgotten friends
Missed donations
Not making amends

Strained relationships
Desensitized to everyone
Emotionless trip
Kindness and empathy none

Emotions scattered
Health in ruin
Definitely battered
Ready to be done in

Life falls apart
Little by little
Leading to a bad heart
So brittle

But I am an associate
Paying taxes and voting
A member of our capitalist state
But I am not gloating

I forgot the truth
I forgot the guidelines
I forgot the nursery rhymes
I forgot the wisdom books

A wealth of knowledge
I learned long ago

I must acknowledge
I did know

Charity
Forgiveness
Compassion
Moderation

Why did I not
Live a life
That I was taught
Without conflict and strife

Was I needy
Was I selfish
Was I greedy
Was I foolish

Yes
I can agree
I made a mess
I was privileged and free

Why did I need more
Why could I not be happy
Why did I war
Why was I snappy

Who cares
All that is gone
Drop your airs
Today is a new dawn

Life is here
And kind
Listen and hear
Open your mind

To another earth
One of jubilation
Allowing a rebirth
Out of damnation

To a life of fraternity
Remembering community
Now and for eternity
My new opportunity

Torment

I do not know
Does it really matter
The ongoing show
Life and dreams in tatter

My brain goes dead
My eyes are hurt by sunlight
My sudden falls I dread
My words are not right

A rare disease
A common anxiety
Just please please
Not so much variety

Give me a concern
Give me a fight
Give me a turn
Give me the right

Right to control
Right to fix
Right to be whole
Right to end the conflicts

Conflicts of doubt
Conflicts of pain
Conflicts to act out
Conflicts of strain

I am tired
What is worse
A life expired
Or alone in the universe

I am not afraid to die
Jesus is there
It is not a lie
In the Lord's care

I afraid to be alone
It is stressful
A great unknown
Very distressful
Why why why
Can I not be content
I want to cry
A great torment

Tormented by what
No human touch
Not clear cut
Or just too much

Do I smother
Do I overwhelm
One after another
Making it my realm

Drive people away
Make them afraid
To share and play

My torments are homemade

I cannot understand
A balanced life together
I demand and demand
All to be hooked by a tether

Can I change
Find a way
To rearrange
My greatest dismay

Confined in solitary
I have friends
We can be merry
But that where it ends

No one to dance
No companionship
No romance
No courtship

I have tried
I have bailed
I have cried
I have failed

It is my fate
To go one more time
Is it too late
To make my life rhyme

Be told
Be courageous
Be bold
It is advantageous

Bore

I am a bore
Very whinny
A word whore
Not funny

Why tell people your troubles
When they got their own
They do not live in a bubble
Or made of stone

They have feelings
And they have needs
Listen to their dealings
And their life deeds

Turn the conversation around
Quit talking about yourself
And your constant frown
Leave your feelings on the shelf

Pour yourself into others
Be a blessing to them
Ask about their brothers and mothers
And what they have overcome

Offer them a prayer
Make it simple and plain
Something they can wear
To reduce their pain

My feelings will improve
Making it about you
A good positive move
Long overdue

Chapter 4 - Family and Friends

There is no love in life than for your friends and family. These are the people who have walked a long time with you. They have made the journey through good and hard times. I have had some friends for 40 years, and I have had my family for 59 years.

Some people guided and advised you for a year or two of your life, but they had an everlasting impression upon your character. I love to write poems for these individuals and to share the verses with them. The poetry might be poor, but it expresses my feelings for these heroes of my life. I hope they realize how much I cherish and honor them.

I hope you envision the love of I have these friends and family members.

Be A Friend

In life, tell a story
In life, share a joke
In life, give God His glory
In life, be a sturdy oak

Treat your friends fair
Forgive your friends
For friends, say many a prayer
Beginning or at the end

For your family and your mother
Hug and love them most
You will meet one after another
But no one like your mother, not close

Be positive with good cheer
Know you are strong
Keep our Father, God near
And sing a happy song

Whistle a happy tune
With a big smile
At noon or under the moon
Make that your style

This beautiful gal
Who is joyful and sunny
A friend and pal
As sweet as honey

Daughter

You are a late boomer
Like a little pup
You will need to work hard
But do not give us
You have marvelous abilities

I have seen your unique talents
Greeting and meeting people
Use those skills

Going up life's steep hill
And you will get there

People want to be loved
What better way than to use their name
I have seen you do it
It will lead to your legendary fame
That girl is kind and polite

These are emotional intelligence
Qualities that cannot be measured
So chase these abilities
And you find treasures
In your lifetime

These traits can be used anywhere
Do not take them for granted
The church, grocery store, or wherever
The talent is planted
In your mind at a young age

Do not stop
Now or forever
This is a Godly blessing
You will prosper and endeavor
By being genuine and generous

Share your emotions
Give others delight
Concentrate on those traits
And you will be shining bright
A shining light for all to see

Family

Do you enjoy
Your family
Or is it a ploy
Or an anomaly

A ploy to get money
A ploy to get affection
A ploy to be funny
A ploy for connection

A connection to what
A connection to who
A connection in my gut
A connection made of glue

Join us together
Fasten us to each other
A common tether
Mother or brother

Is this common
Is this normal
Is this unusual
Is this irregular

No it is not
For many to live
Relatives not forgot
Families to thrive

What is the common thread
Families to proceed
Is it the homestead
Or the blood of a family creed

A creed to love
A creed to support
A creed to encourage
A creed to equally share

Generation to generation
Forgive one another
Give for the duration
Smother and smother

Smother with love
Smother with kindness
Smother with resources
Smother with mercy

Mercy is the hardest
When we feel wronged
But we can harness
By remembering we belonged

Belonged to a family line
Belonged to a congregation
Belonged to the vine
Belonged to a narration

A narration to work together
A narration to read

A narration to learn
A narration to believe

Believe in God
Believe in kin
Believe all are flawed
Believe we all sin

Sin is there
Every single day
Repent with prayer
Believe and pray

God is first
Family second
Our nation third
And there is no fourth

Align on one
Read the one
Learn the one
Worship the one

Forgive those in two
Love those in two
Show mercy to those in two
Share with those in two

Honor those in three
Respect those in three
Support those in three
Affirm those in three

Teach yours these
Time and time again
These are the keys
Our family will remain

Atlanta

Looking searching
For someone very rare
Online researching
To make a pair

The process is rude
Taking a lot of time
Matchmaking is crude
A steep road to climb

Uphill forward uphill
Up I climb and I go
Like Jack and Jill
Rolling back down below

It is a rough rocky trip
No responses and old photos
Requires statesmanship
Is it worth then who knows

I do know indeed I do
When a match is made
I am no longer blue
Answer to the words I prayed

An independent woman
Raising three boys
Her whole adult lifespan
With great strength and poise

She can hold a conversation
Sharing her feelings
Adding banter and flirtation
In all our dealings

She is deliciously funny
Using humorous jest
Making her attitude sunny
Her words suggest

She likes to dance
On her kitchen tile floor
I have learned in advance
Enabling my spirit to soar

Here is a gal
Who is having fun
Maybe I can be her pal
And be her someone

Slow down slow down
You have never met
Please do not frown
Or do not fret

Enjoy the time together
Enjoy the little moments
Enjoy the phone calls
Enjoy her presence

God is in control
God will do His thing

I know my role
I know my King

God wants the best
For you and me
We are rewarded and blessed
Let us celebrate Gods jubilee

God will pick a day
For us to meet
Boardgames we will play
Empathic in your defeat

Speed Dating

How do you meet someone
For the very first time
So you have a little fun
And your personalities rhyme

Go through the dating ritual
First date dinner and a movie
Second date dinner and a movie
And third date dinner and a movie

Fourth date maybe a kiss
Fifth date maybe hold hands
Sixth date maybe meet the family
Seventh date maybe go to church

Eighth date blah blah blah
Ninth date wore out
Tenth date ready to quit
Dating takes perseverance and energy

But what if in three days
You go through nine to ten dates
Saving yourself months and months
Predictable tedious ritual

Almost impossible
I do have to say
No way possible
Not children play

I am here to exclaim
Anything can happen
When you are older
And done the marriage thing

We met online
Talked and talked
Did not dine
Date or walked

We were miles apart
Living our lives
Filling our own shopping cart
Not missing our past husbands or wives

We had done that bit
And it was not rewarding
I had used all my wit
To block those recordings

I wanted a friend
I wanted a buddy
I wanted a companion
I wanted a partner

I am a believer in Christ
I am a good person
I am a theist
My situation could not worsen

By myself
Living day to day

Living life from the bookshelf
I did pray and pray

God would provide
On His timetable
Before I died
A one of a kind love fable

Was I desperate
Was I needy
Was I lonely
Was I empty

Maybe
Maybe not
Not a baby
Not with fraught

Opportunity or chance
Presented itself
Beach trip for romance
To satisfy ourselves

What to lose
Except for a beautiful day at the beach
Without the blues
Present your case and beseech

Implore her to meet
Take a road trip
To sun fun and eat
Does anyone give a flip

We are mature
Christ is our guide
We can be pure
Take everything in stride

So we did
Met for a short vacation
And it was good
No frustration

We sat in the sand
Walked along the shore
And tanned and tanned
Traveled to the grocery store

We shared a few meals
We shared a few laughs
We shared our thoughts
We shared our feelings

Attended church
Built a complicated puzzle
Did our research
I never had to wear a muzzle

Chill our magic word
If we needed a timeout
Which was never heard
We did not go that route

We told our secrets and mysteries

Taking a gigantic risk
Of course shared our histories
Information to fill a disc

Time went fast
Unbelievably quick
Three days went past
We made a girl flick

No problems
Separate bedrooms
No misgivings or regrets
Sincerity and respect

In less than seventy two hours
We had met and lived
Half a year
In normal dating progression

Now what
Where do we go
In my gut
Just go with the flow

God is in control
God is our leader
Not living by a poll
But I do need her

She was smart
She was a Christian
She was witty and quick

She was gorgeous and beautiful

Patience is the key
Let God prepare the way
We both agree
We cannot stray

I am delighted
To meet a wonderful female
God had provided
To glorify this fable or tale

Thank you God
You are the best
I am awed
And blessed

People In Your Life

People come and go
Part of our life
And it is so
Some through strife

Harder for some
To keep it together
Always so dumb
Bad or fair weather

Prideful
Arrogant
Selfish
Belligerent

To name a few

But more to ask for
If you care to view
Here are more

Life circumstances
Life traumas
Life illnesses
Life mysteries

All kinds of reasons
To be a jerk
In all seasons
To go berserk

How you act
Is how you are framed
Try to use tact
Or you get blamed

You cannot hide
For exceptionally long
Sooner or later you slide
You are not that strong

To keep it at bay
To keep it hidden
To keep it suppressed
To keep it smothered

Useless effort
Try to isolate
To be better

Is one trait

Force others away
So be by yourself
No one to play
Just pictures on the shelf

A lonely crutch
To protect your outbursts
People are too much
These are not unique firsts

Social distancing
Endless therapy
Countless medicines
Retreats and asylums

Doctors galore
Psychobabble
What a bore
Good for the rabble

But the worse cases
Must be dumbed down
See it in their faces
The emotionless frowns

Pump them with drugs
To make them acceptable
No longer thugs
Almost respectable

They might be slow
They might drool
They might be lazy
They might be dim

But they are tamed
They can be presented
And beautifully framed
Sat in the corner ornamented

I do not want to be dampened
I do not want to be unnoticed
I do not want to be a simpleton
I do not want to be devalued

But to live in peace
To live with immunity
To live it must cease
To live in unity

Cease the anger
Cease the explosion
Cease the banter
Cease the implosion

Make a choice
Or stay in a cave
And listen to your own voice
And be your own slave

George Harrison

Too many good men
In my life
I take to paper and pen
To declare with drum and fife

They lived next door
In my favorite town
Poquoson was no bore
My favorite place hands down

Mr Harrison taught me many things
And he spent time with me
He helped expand my wings
And all his instruction was free

The main thing I learned
Was how to sail
And right the boat when overturned
When there was a terrific gale

But not only on the ocean
In life too
Mr Harrison had a sense of promotion
He was very ever blue

He enjoyed himself
I watched him every day
Take toys off the shelf
He liked to play

Sailing
Fishing
Traveling
Living

He was far different than most
Not a care in the world
Or he kept them close
And did not let them whirl

Probably another good example
If you want to know the truth
Another sample
From my youth
Not him alone
His wife included
The most caring woman I have known
I have concluded

Memories and recollections
Have vast they are
Great reflections
I will never forget by far

Dale Treadway

Mr Treadway a good mam
A man to be missed
He had a plan
And he did exist

He left me one truth
I do not know if anyone knew
From my youth
Mr Treadways worldview

Working in my backyard
We talked of business
My businesses marred
And here came his wiseness

Mr Treadway asked me
Are you a believer in Christ
Yes I try to be
A good theist

He pushed me deeper
Is it the most important thing for you
Are you a Bible truth keeper
And Mr Treadway gave me a clue

A clue to life
A clue to worth
A clue to follow
A clue to pursue

He gave me examples
People who have strived
By attending Bible classes
And their lives revived

I did not repent that day
I did not turn to God
I did not sing hallelujah
I did not fall to my knees

But his words
Changed my path
In two years
Repent I did
His words spurred
Paved my way
Along with others conferred
The Gospel is not childs play

I found the Lord
I found a better journey
I found a Savior
I found everlasting peace

Thank you
For your sincere instruction
Definitely it is the glue
To my reproduction

Not perfect
Not the best
Not faultless

Not ideal

But a true believer
So so rigorous
With Holy Spirit fever
To be so vigorous

Jim Linberg

He was my boss
I met him young
Color gloss or semigloss
What was his color

He was strong
He was smart
He was energetic
He was old

Old at sixteen
Anyone over twenty
We were green
Years to come aplenty

He taught us much
Too much to list
Always there in a clutch
Able to assist

A great role model
A great friend
Would not let you dawdle
Or lead down a dead end

We were kids
And we still played
Just lift your eyelids
And do not be afraid

See and envision
Badminton galore
Buckets of beer
In his backyard

So much fun
But the best
It cannot be outdone
More significant than all the rest

Zoom Schwartz Profigliano
We sang these words
No not soprano
But as songbirds

To each other
Around a table
As each other's brother
This is not a fable

He taught us leadership
He taught us friendship
He taught us hard work
He taught us to rhyme and balance

Time for fun and toil
Time for love
Time to spoil
Time for Him above

God was not manifest
During these times

As we followed our zest
But now in our primes

We see each other at church
Talk of God
No need to search
Neither is a fraud

Poquoson was there
So many life impressions
And with glorious prayer
He taught the best sessions

Elizabeth

Elizabeth is fun
Elizabeth is smart
Elizabeth is the one
Who likes to fart

She is comical and funny
She is lovable and sweet
She is bright and sunny
She is a unique and special treat

She brightens your day

With her energy and heart
And you do not want her to get away
She is like a beautiful piece of art

But she has her race
Her place in the sun
And she needs her space
So she can run

My prayer is you read
And have God as your friend
Let Him lead you
Until the very end

Chapter 5 - Love

The one emotion that makes your whole life different. Your life is unique and exclusive. Your life has security and expression. Another person enjoys your company, and they commit to being part of your life.

I had one person in my life who cared and nurtured me. They entertained me. We laughed
bunches, and we loved exclusively.

A wonderful time with this person and a person who I will be fond of forever.

Leigh

You make me feel alive
You make me dream
You allow me to thrive
You make me scream

I enjoy you
I find you desirable
I really really knew
I knew you were adorable

What does this mean
Where do we go
Who is the pretty queen
When do we grow

You queen are in control
I compliment you
I know my role
One of your crew

But my role is unique
Giving you passion
Or what you seek
With compassion

Personally I think
You provide a great kiss
Our passions sync
Providing so much bliss

Patience is king
Time will tell
If this is a fling
Or it can swell

Who will break
Whose heart
Or make one ache
Or fall apart

I do not know
I have no clue
I go with the flow
What is your view

You or me
Does it matter

We are individuals and free
To choose to stop the chatter

If we quit laughing
Or quit listening
Or courtesy lacking
Our mood stiffening

That will be it
No reason to plead
We need just to quit
At great speed

Time is treasured
Something is wrong
Life is measured
But for how long

You are steady but weak
I am not diagnosed
Both train wrecks
A tie almost

I know my thoughts
Easy sailing in fair weather
Just connect the dots
We will stay together

Is it serious
To me yes
Very very delirious
A great success

To Leigh
It is crazy
Cannot agree
All very hazy

Have you hit your head
I do not think so
Think about what you said
And say it slow

I am head over heel
To be your lover
And to me it real
So let me discover

Do we have a chance
Is there a way
For me to romance
You for the rest of our days

Love

I am so in love with you
You are so smart
And this is not untrue
You seized my heart

Long ago
I was smitten
Learned to flow
And fit in

Not easy to suppress
My A personality
Like a game of chess
In the chase totality

You are pretty

Very stunning
And very witty
I am not running

A diamond lost
That I have found
No matter the cost
I am bound

I want to set it
In my life
I have to admit
As my wife

I Am What I Am

I have some poor skills
I am not the best
I want thrills
I will do my best

Massage is too fast
Like scurrying about
But I have a zest
And will figure it out

My technique was poor
Very unskilled and inept
No images of grandeur
But do not have to accept

I can practice
And listen
Turn from a cactus
To one which glistens

To please you
To enjoy our life
Give you your due
As my wife

Honor and cherish
Sing your praises
My love will not perish
Fire for you blazes

Love Grows

I am so excited
You are for me
I am delighted
I think you agree

The little touches
The time together
Keep me in your clutches
In all types of weather

Do not get upset
Over little things
Or fret
When life swings

Let us live
Day by day
I want to give
And to play

Share my heart
To be your love
Give every part
Parts undreamed of

Take care of you
Care about your wholeness
And when you are blue
Relieve your hopelessness

I am sure
My love is true
I can assure
My heart overflows too

My heart grows
Because I care
I want and choose
You are so precious and rare

Adore

What is adore
How do we get there
Not a story of lore
But let me share

It starts as a nightingale
A crush on a caregiver
A common tale
To someone who can deliver

Smart Girl worked hard
To analyze me
Another patient on her dance card
She is my significant key

She found I walk funny
She sent me to a specialist
She was so sunny
She was excellent

I found her smart
I found her pretty
I found her a piece of art
I found her witty

Yes they fixed my pain
My leg quit hurting
Adverting the ball and chain
Now my interest was flirting

I asked her out
Once or twice
A difficult route
But worth the price

It took weeks and weeks
To win her over
Through valleys and peaks
She was a rover

A single mother
She has medical challenges
No men and does not want another
She just wants to keep her life in balance

I was not deterred
I was smitten
I was stirred
I needed to fit in

I met her needs
Little acts of kindness
Many small deeds
Growing our fondness

We talked and talked
We played and played
We shared and shared
We gave and gave

Life took off
We lived mightily

Enjoying life from a trough
We were a family

We ate dinner together
We walked the dog
We attended school events
We went on trips

She improved my condition
Reducing my stress
Eliminating my strange emission
Making my symptoms much less

Our lives proceeded
For a long time
Warning signs were unheeded
We had reached our prime

She had to choose
Old life or new
Two different views
Which one is true

I did not help
Wanting my way
All ended in a yelp
And a fray

I was frustrated
She was smothered
All issues debated
She was mothered

She was safe
She was secure
She was loved
She was dandy

No reason to change
No reason to move
No reason to exchange
No reason to improve

Our lives deteriorated
Too hard to maintain
I was patient and waited
Living through the strain

Talk and talk
Going to transform
Waiting out the clock
And get through the storm

I needed her
She nurtured me
I wanted her
She understood me

But it was not to be
Our love did not last
We lost our glee
Our lives were in the past

No new memories

No new adventures
No new experiences
No new experiments

My heart was broken
I was incredibly sad
She had spoken
Again a nomad

On my own
Living life
Life alone
No community strife

Just circumstances
Circumstances of anxiousness
Circumstances of nervousness
Circumstances of restiveness

This went on for a while
A routine of existence
Peaceful in exile
Not much resistance

The text came
For us to unite
Back in the game
Everything alright

We had not changed
Back to our truths
Nothing rearranged

Back to our youths

Playing ball
Going to pool
Watching movies
Holding hands

We had missed some days
We had not seen each other
We had made it through the haze
We had ended the pother

Smart Girl found a disorder
Sounding like my quirks
Almost like a hoarder
Of crazy weird works

I was diagnosed with it
How exciting and fresh
But it fit
I keep my pound of flesh

No death sentence
How grand
Learn tools of repentance
Tools to manage my land

Land of coziness
Land of familiarity
Land of closeness
Land of comradeliness

Journey back to the word
Adore worship admire
Love esteem honor preferred
My heart on fire

Unexpectantly
Our lives interrupted
Our future and destiny
Everything disrupted

Disrupted our utopia
Where do we go
Entering dystopia
We will not grow

Back to the same place
A prison of sorts
Not our own space
Our life distorts

Too many chiefs
Too many frustrations
Too many rules
Too many debates

We are a couple
It is up to us
Not very supple
Just more fuss

Hard enough with one
But two or three

Along with intentional shun
We will not be free

I want to respect
I want to admire
I want to cherish
I want to honor

I want to get along
I want to go with the flow
I want to be strong
I want to be in the show

But it has to be her and me
Our lives and decisions
We must unify and agree
To enjoy our vision

I gave up hope
Thinking it was done
Walking the tightrope
No life in the long run

She had made her choice
Months ago
I heard her voice
I was a useless cargo

I was expendable
I was a throwaway
I was undefendable
I was a cliche

Moody
Crazy
Unstable
Wacky

Yes it is correct
I am not perfect
Last time I checked
But then she picked

She picked love
She picked romance
She picked affection
She picked one to kiss

She likes our playfulness
She likes our secureness
She likes our tenderness
She likes our togetherness

Adore is here
In all its glory
Shout and hear
Our great story

We have fun
And laugh
We have joy
And happiness

Adore is a journey

A road to travel
A grand tourney
Let us not unravel

Sailing the Lee

I have sailed
Along the lee shore
Sometimes jailed
A situation not to ignore

I cannot escape
The wind pushing me hard
Unable to make my sail shape
Act quick or my boat scarred

Wrecked upon the rocks
Wrecked upon the reef
Wrecked upon the shoal
Wrecked upon the beach

Why keep the boat

Why not swim away
Why not jump and float
Why not go your way

I hate to leave my vessel
A good looking ship
Easy to sail and wrestle
Wrestle and ride on a trip

Or wasting my life
Hoping to reach or tack
To a safe point with no strife
With the wind to my back

But where is the fun
Where is the excitement
A blast compared to none
Enticement and incitement

Close hauled along the edge
Water breaking over the bow
I have not hedged or pledged
To give up and quit now

Flying through the water
The boat lifted high
There is a breakwater
Safety is nearby

But why oh why
Do I reduce sail
Or tack and glide by

Using the gale

I will miss the challenge
I will miss my love
I will miss the satisfaction
I will miss the gratification

There is nothing like her
There is nothing to compare
There are emotions to stir
There are moments to share

I plan to sail on
Catching the wind
Until the emotion is gone
Or just left behind

Behind in the docks
Or on its trailer
Or sitting on blocks
Missing its sailor

All About Today

I am not sure or know
If I will waste away and die
Every day go with the flow
Daily just soar and fly

Fly like a bird
Enjoy the ride
Move ever forward
Take life in stride

Stride day by day
One day at a time
Merriment and play
A life that will rhyme

Rhyme requires two
Words that go together
Why can it not be you
To get me through bad weather

I know I know another place
And another time it is not right
But I want to see your face
Side by side through this fight

A companion buddy sidekick
Who enjoys the journey
And we are familiar and klick
Through many tourneys

We are familiar
We are comfortable
We are known
We are snug

Yes it can be hard
I can be frustrated
Leaving you scarred
With words I have stated

But you are not perfect
Ignoring and hurting me
Increasing the conflict
But let us agree to disagree

All the naming and blaming
It is a waste of energy and strength
I am proclaiming and exclaiming
I will go through any length

To apologize and to repent
I am so sad
Because it is not my hearts intent
To be so mean and bad

You may not trust me
And want me back
It is your choice to be free
If there was a tiny crack

Where we could amend

Our life dreams
My best friend
I wish it is our theme

A theme of love
A theme of us
A theme of care
A theme of respect

All of the good things
Life demands
As we soar on our wings
Over the badlands

We fly in unity
Twisting and turning
Searching for opportunities
For our lifes yearnings

Soaring higher and higher
Flying unrestricted and liberated
I hear the angels choir
Beautiful and orchestrated

Enjoy the glorious songs
On journeys we navigate
Easing and erasing our wrongs
From our first to our last date

Marriage

You must believe
To care for the truth
And perceive
God from our youth

The Bible is true
The Bible is correct
The Bible is glue
The Bible is perfect

If you do not believe in God
Or in the truth of the Bible
This poem is a wad
Of foolish trifle

So stop here
Do not read another verse
You will not hear
The truth of the universe

To be unyoked
To ugly darkness
You will be provoked
By its starkness

But not by Gods light
Which shines on us all
Bright as Gods image
We do get the call

To share in Gods plan
Told in the Bibles first book
Genesis is where it began
Let us take a look

A man should not be alone
No helper found fit
God made women almost a clone
One flesh closely knit

God made an equal member
Two is better than one
Let us remember
Ecclesiastes is how it is spun

Gods plan is guy and gal

And he did not want us by ourselves
And they say we shall
Put all emotions on the shelf

On the shelf of love
On the shelf of encouragement
On the shelf of self sacrifice
On the shelf of commitment

God knew the world was fallen
And the world was hard
Most would fall in
You need to stand guard

Horrible things occur
To Gods creation
We must concur
It does not fit Gods narration

A narration of obedience
A narration of contentment
A narration of joy
A narration of peace

Why can we not stand up
To the evil in the world
The devils evil cup
As the devils world whirls

Whirls around us
Challenging our loyalties
Creating lots of fuss

Stealing our royalties

Royalties of forgiveness
Royalties of life
Royalties of heaven
Royalties of God

To challenge the evil miscarriages
God gave us each other
Man and female in marriages
Christians as a sister and a brother

A sister and brother
A brother and brother
A sister and sister
A brother and sister

To protect one another
To encourage one another
To carry one another
To help one another

In this fallen place
It is a mighty wonder
There is Gods grace
We can fall under

We sin immensely
In many ways
Most intensely
Setting God ablaze

Same sex marriage, divorce
Lies, gossip, small talk
Which ones to enforce
It is all a crock

They are all sin
Hated by God
We cannot win
We are all frauds

God knew
God gave us a rope
God came through
God gave us hope

We are not done
God sent Jesus to die
He sent his son
To ransom and buy

Our sinful mouths
Our sinful eyes
Our sinful trespasses
Our sinful lives

Just believe
Jesus is Lord
God rose Jesus
From the dead

It is not tough
Just repent

Call the devils bluff
A life changing event

A new journey
A new body
A new understanding
A new standing

Not easy
Never is
Can get sleazy
Do not fizz

You have made it
To Gods mysteries
You do not need your wit
Just Holy Spirit victories

Victories in choices
Victories in prayer
Victories in service
Victories in churches

Celebrate today
A new life view
This is the way
For me and you

Notes:

Belief
Acts:22-31 English Standard Version (ESV)

Paul Addresses the Areopagus 22 So Paul, standing in the midst of the Areopagus, said: "Men of Athens, I perceive that in every way you are very religious. 23 For as I passed along and observed the objects of your worship, I found also an altar with this inscription: 'To the unknown god.' What therefore you worship as unknown, this I proclaim to you. 24 The God who made the world and everything in it, being Lord of heaven and earth, does not live in temples made by man,[a] 25 nor is he served by human hands, as though he needed anything, since he himself gives to all mankind life and breath and everything. 26 And he made from one man every nation of mankind to live on all the face of the earth, having determined allotted periods and the boundaries of their dwelling place, 27 that they should seek God, and perhaps feel their way toward him and find him. Yet he is actually not far from each one of us, 28 for "'In him we live and move and have our being';[b] as even some of your own poets have said, "'For we are indeed his offspring.'[c] 29 Being then God's offspring, we ought not to think that the divine being is like gold or silver or stone, an image formed by the art and imagination of man. 30 The times of ignorance God overlooked, but now he commands all people everywhere to repent, 31 because he has fixed a day on which he will judge the world in righteousness by a man whom he has appointed; and of this he has given assurance to all by raising him from the dead."

2 Peter 1:20-21 English Standard Version (ESV)
20 knowing this first of all, that no prophecy of Scripture comes from someone's own interpretation. 21 For no

prophecy was ever produced by the will of man, but men spoke from God as they were carried along by the Holy Spirit.

Unyoked

2 Corinthians 6:14 English Standard Version (ESV)
The Temple of the Living God 14 Do not be unequally yoked with unbelievers. For what partnership has righteousness with lawlessness? Or what fellowship has light with darkness?

God's Image

Genesis 1:26-27 English Standard Version (ESV)
26 Then God said, "Let us make man[a] in our image, after our likeness. And let them have dominion over the fish of the sea and over the birds of the heavens and over the livestock and over all the earth and over every creeping thing that creeps on the earth."
27 So God created man in his own image,
in the image of God he created him;
male and female he created them.

God's Plan

Genesis 2:18-24 English Standard Version (ESV)
18 Then the LORD God said, "It is not good that the man should be alone; I will make him a helper fit for[a] him." 19 Now out of the ground the LORD God had formed[b] every beast of the field and every bird of the heavens and brought them to the man to see what he would call them. And whatever the man called every

living creature, that was its name. 20 The man gave names to all livestock and to the birds of the heavens and to every beast of the field. But for Adam[c] there was not found a helper fit for him. 21 So the LORD God caused a deep sleep to fall upon the man, and while he slept took one of his ribs and closed up its place with flesh. 22 And the rib that the LORD God had taken from the man he made[d] into a woman and brought her to the man. 23 Then the man said,
"This at last is bone of my bones
and flesh of my flesh;
she shall be called Woman,
because she was taken out of Man."[e]
24 Therefore a man shall leave his father and his mother and hold fast to his wife, and they shall become one flesh.

Why two is better than one

Ecclesiastes 4:9-12 English Standard Version (ESV)
9 Two are better than one, because they have a good reward for their toil. 10 For if they fall, one will lift up his fellow. But woe to him who is alone when he falls and has not another to lift him up! 11 Again, if two lie together, they keep warm, but how can one keep warm alone? 12 And though a man might prevail against one who is alone, two will withstand him—a threefold cord is not quickly broken.

Hebrews 10:24-25 And let us consider how we may spur one another on toward love and good deeds, not giving up meeting together, as some are in the habit of doing,

but encouraging one another—and all the more as you see the Day approaching.
Philippians 2:3-4 Do nothing from selfish ambition or conceit, but in humility count others more significant than yourselves. Let each of you look not only to his own interests, but also to the interests of others.
Romans 15:1 We who are strong ought to bear with the failings of the weak and not to please ourselves.
Galatians 6:2 Carry each other's burdens, and in this way you will fulfill the law of Christ.
Hebrews 13:1-2 Keep on loving one another as brothers and sisters. Do not forget to show hospitality to strangers, for by so doing some people have shown hospitality to angels without knowing it.
Romans 12:5 so in Christ we, though many, form one body, and each member belongs to all the others.
Corinthians 12:14 Yes, the body has many different parts, not just one part.
Corinthians 12:20-21 As it is, there are many parts, but one body. The eye cannot say to the hand, "I don't need you!" And the head cannot say to the feet, "I don't need you!"

Warnings for being alone

Proverbs 18:1 English Standard Version (ESV)
18 Whoever isolates himself seeks his own desire;
he breaks out against all sound judgment.

Psalm 72:12 English Standard Version (ESV)
12 For he delivers the needy when he calls,
the poor and him who has no helper.

1 Peter 5:8 Be sober-minded; be watchful. Your adversary the devil prowls around like a roaring lion, seeking someone to devour.
Genesis 4:7 If you do what is right, will you not be accepted? But if you do not do what is right, sin is crouching at your door; it desires to have you, but you must rule over it.
Romans 7:21 So I find this law at work: Although I want to do good, evil is right there with me.
1 Thessalonians 5:14 And we urge you, brothers and sisters, warn those who are idle and disruptive, encourage the disheartened, help the weak, be patient with everyone.

Single is possible under the right conditions

1 Corinthians 7:8-9 English Standard Version (ESV)
8 To the unmarried and the widows I say that it is good for them to remain single, as I am. 9 But if they cannot exercise self-control, they should marry. For it is better to marry than to burn with passion.

Marriage
Ephesians 5:22-33 English Standard Version (ESV)
Wives and Husbands
22 Wives, submit to your own husbands, as to the Lord. 23 For the husband is the head of the wife even as Christ is the head of the church, his body, and is himself its Savior. 24 Now as the church submits to Christ, so also wives should submit in everything to their husbands.
25 Husbands, love your wives, as Christ loved the church and gave himself up for her, 26 that he might

sanctify her, having cleansed her by the washing of water with the word, 27 so that he might present the church to himself in splendor, without spot or wrinkle or any such thing, that she might be holy and without blemish.[a] 28 In the same way husbands should love their wives as their own bodies. He who loves his wife loves himself. 29 For no one ever hated his own flesh, but nourishes and cherishes it, just as Christ does the church, 30 because we are members of his body. 31 "Therefore a man shall leave his father and mother and hold fast to his wife, and the two shall become one flesh." 32 This mystery is profound, and I am saying that it refers to Christ and the church. 33 However, let each one of you love his wife as himself, and let the wife see that she respects her husband.

Why does marriages fail?

Sin and pride in this world

Are divorces what God wants?

Hebrews 13:4 English Standard Version (ESV)
4 Let marriage be held in honor among all, and let the marriage bed be undefiled, for God will judge the sexually immoral and adulterous.
Mark 10 English Standard Version (ESV)

Teaching About Divorce

Mark 10:1-10 And he left there and went to the region of Judea and beyond the Jordan, and crowds gathered to him again. And again, as was his custom, he taught them.

2 And Pharisees came up and in order to test him asked, "Is it lawful for a man to divorce his wife?" 3 He answered them, "What did Moses command you?" 4 They said, "Moses allowed a man to write a certificate of divorce and to send her away." 5 And Jesus said to them, "Because of your hardness of heart he wrote you this commandment. 6 But from the beginning of creation, 'God made them male and female.' 7 'Therefore a man shall leave his father and mother and hold fast to his wife,[a] 8 and the two shall become one flesh.' So they are no longer two but one flesh. 9 What therefore God has joined together, let not man separate."

10 And in the house the disciples asked him again about this matter. 11 And he said to them, "Whoever divorces his wife and marries another commits adultery against her, 12

And if she divorces her husband and marries another, she commits adultery."

Chapter 6 – Grief and Sorrow

Love takes you to one side of your emotions but breaking up and fighting take you to the other side of those emotions. I have experienced many times in my life, but this break-up devastates my soul.

I want this person in my life, I want this person to last forever, and I want this person to be my partner, friend, companion, confidant, buddy, and lover. When these dreams break down, it leads to despair. I am not hopeless that I will fall apart or my life will end. I despair that there was a person that I enjoyed very much. A person who made me laugh, and I made her laugh. A person who tried so very hard to be my friend.

These poems record my loss, my grief, and my struggle. Also, these verses emphasize the bargaining I endured to make myself good with our relationship crashing to the ground. I was self-talking Where I tried to encourage myself that all will be good or all was good. In my heart, I know I gave all I could give. I made mistakes, but they were not deal busters. I guess that is part of my sorrow. I did not feel like I deserved to be treated this way. But does that really matter?

The one thing I have learned over the past 59 years is that life is not fair. One of life's greatest lessons is to learn to deal with these unpleasant events in your life. My poem, My Dance , explains this waltz moving from happiness to sadness how you can live through most adversity by flowing with your troubles. I wish that I had learned this when I was a kid. I was too rigid, I was too unaware of life injustices, and I was naive — what a surprise.

I hope you enjoy the poems and you can feel my pain and grief.

Heart Ache

Kick and scream
Find exceptions
Lessen our dream
Create deceptions

No one is perfect
Not one
We are wrecked
It cannot be undone

I drown
You suffocate
Just calm down
We do not need to frustrate

Somewhere
Somehow
It is rare
The here and now

Live today
One step at a time
We can enter the fray
Just climb

With our disabilities
Up the hill
Sharing our capabilities
To fulfill

Each other
Give more than take
Loving one another
Think about what we can make

A relationship
to encourage
A membership
to nourish

A healthy life
For us
Not strife
No fuss

Friendship
Not ownership
Partnership
Not dictatorship

Someone to share
Time and space
Morning prayer
And lots of grace

Someone to say hello
Goodbye
Make us know
We satisfy

This is not about intercourse
It is past

Our driving force
Is companionship at last

Share a meal
Watch it snow
Travel in a fifth wheel
Or play the banjo

The sky is the limit
When we journey together
Enjoy it
No matter the weather.

Done

I will not accept
You are done
I have not wept
You are the one

I love you
You love me
It is not new
And it is not free

We must work
To keep our love
Do not go berserk
Or give it a shove

Life can be hard
It can be scary
Stay on guard
Stay wary

Easy to get discouraged
Overwhelmed by worry
Just stay encouraged
Avoid the awful flurry

We belong together
A good life awaits
Fairweather
A blissful state

Fun fun fun
Many years ahead
Enjoy our time in the sun
And leave nothing unsaid

Grateful

I do not know why
I feel so blue
I want to cry
It is true

I spin my wheels
Not getting started
No completing deals
Everything halfhearted

I have a girlfriend
Who I love
In the end
Marriage or kind of

I have a business chance
Maybe two or three
It is a dance
Work smart and advance

I have a silver spoon
Not worried about it
It is an easy tune
Spoiled I have to admit

I found a house
It is very nice
For my spouse
At a good price

I have many friends
Who I love dearly
With them life transcends
Seeing them yearly

I have a special girl
Who makes me laugh
She is a precious pearl
Still such a little calf

My belief
Is true
What a relief
Definitely my worldview

What is my deal
I spin and spin
Is it real
Or is it built-in

My mind races
Around and around
Not receiving graces
Bleeding from my wound

It is in my head
Not a safe place
I dread and dread
Empty space

Alone

No one home
Not known
Just roam

Ignored
Adrift
Lord oh Lord
Give me a lift

I know the story
I know the truth
I know your glory
It takes no sleuth

You are the way
You are my hope
Just pray
Reach for the rope

Grab Him
Remind yourself
Sing a hymn
Get the Bible off the shelf

It is all so easy
An easy process
It is not cheesy
Not a game of chess

Love easily
Forgive greatly
Celebrate joyfully
Live bravely

Most of all
Be thankful
Life miseries are small
Gratitude is the mantle

Grief to Life

Why do I grieve
I gave it my all
Rewarded with a reprieve
To stand alone and tall

Reprieve from stress
Walking on eggshells
A game of chess
With no wedding bells

More money
To spend every day
Milk and honey
Spend it my way

Travel the world
Sights to see
Twirl and whirl
I am free

Drugless
My mind works
I must confess
These are perks

Write my rhyming verse
Create and produce thought
I have beaten the curse
No more brain rot

Not drugged dumb
As a mindless ghoul
I have overcome
The ceaseless drool

But is it all that great
To have all this
Without a mate
To hug and kiss

This is why I mourn
I have lost my buddy
Our love torn
My heart muddy

I am so conflicted
So many upsides
I am unrestricted
But a ferocious tide

So may extremes
A passionate obsession
I had so many dreams
And a confession

I miss her
She was unique
A sweet liqueur
An aura of mystique

There will be no one like her

No one to replace our fun
I miss being her chauffeur
But we are done

She sees no need
For a sidekick
Independent and freed
She is her own chick

And this is life
Not very equitable and fair
Without a wonderful wife
And a journey to share

A treacherous fate
To be alone
Which I do hate
Nearing my gravestone

No reason to seek
Another to share
I am past my peak
Along with my wear and tear

Enjoy the positives
And all their good yields
Eliminate the negatives
And their battlefields

Slow down
Stay true
Do not frown

Or turn blue

The easiest way to enjoy
What time is unexpended
Be good and a kind boy
As God intended

Hope and Expectations

Dare I raise my hope
Or raise my expectations
Set me up to be a dope
How about the flirtations

Do I expect her to realize
We are made for each other
And I am better than most guys
Why do I want to bother

To beg her forgiveness
To seek her approval
To deduce her restiveness
To change her disproval

Push her to decide
To spend time with me
Is it mine and her pride
Which is the key

Or is it stupidity
To keep on hoping
When she demonstrates lividity

And I am just coping

I miss our time together
She says the same
How can we tether
Our mutual claim

Leave her alone
Live your life
She has a phone
No more strife

Strife in myself
Strife in her actions
Strife in our childness
Strife in the whole thing

I know we would have fun
We are so good just us
Why does it have to be done
What is the real fuss

I do not know
Questioning her decision
Creating a senseless row
A gigantic collision

She is in control
So let her go
And make some goals
Just go with the flow

Not your best suit
To play it by ear
It might be the best route
Learn to be a seer

Able to visualize
What decisions are best
There may be a prize
If I passed the test

No matter what
My life will be less
But not in a rut
Just some distress

So what is it
Hope that is confused
Expectations that fit
Reconciliation refused

Or is it craziness
To let it rule
Making me melancholy
So stop being a fool

Change

I need a change
To make me whole
Why exchange
My current role

I am not appreciated
I am a man child
I am depressed and deflated
I am forgotten in exile

I have an opinion
I keep to myself
Just a tiny minion
Not being myself

I need to stand up
But then I am immature
And we breakup
And there is no cure

I can walk away
What does it prove
To exit the fray
As my opening move

But this is hard
I am weak going to ground
Getting lonely and scared
Growing lifeless and down

Will I miss my buddy
Just waiting and moping
Way too demanding and bloody
Just hoping

I wish it could be
A life with her
I have made my plea
She does not concur

Instead of pouting
And being blue
Your life needs rerouting
To make it through

Concentrate on me
Setting new priorities
I am single and free
With no authorities

I am off my medication
Planning to travel
Not a vacation
Just to unravel

My mind and thoughts
Through reading and writing
Connecting the dots
And keep on fighting

Fighting for what is right
Which can be a debate
Not worth the bite
I am not a piece of bait

I am not a fish or insect
I am a strong man
I stand erect
I need a plan

Get my health straight
And create multiple verses
Remove dead weight
Solve any reverses

What needs to shift
To execute your plan
Become a spendthrift
And a lousy food ban

Walk even if it hurts
A health goal
And do not chase skirts
So you keep control

Do not be in a rush
Solve all concerns
Work through the slush
And reap the returns

The goodwill produced
Relations restored
I will get a needed boost
Along with an excellent reward

My plan will be ready
To shift my gaze
And to be steady
Through this new phase

Retreat and Rout

I make too many assumptions
Which never work out
Maybe mixed presumptions
Ending in retreat and a rout

Putting everything into one thing
All my energy and emotions
For a yearlong romantic fling
Going through all the motions

The regular dating routines
And a few extra duties
Including helping to clean
Anything for my beauties

I became a caregiver

Helping out with carpools
Even cleaning the silver
Anything for my jewels

I taught after school
Doing weekly reading by committee
Helping enforce the daily rules
Anything for my pretties

Little physical chores
Picking up and putting up the plates
Even cleaning out drawers
Anything for my playmates

But in the long run
It does not matter
All is undone
A gigantic shatter

We break apart
Because there is no solution
The same problem from the start
A matter of the heart

Not really love
Honor and cherish
More push and shove
Close to nightmarish

Warning signs are there
I was a dope
Our relationship not fair
A sense of false hope

Hope for a friend
Hope for a companion
Hope for a sweetheart
Hope for love

I wanted it too much
I would do anything
For someone to touch
For a body to cling

Not her fault

I made the choice
Not to halt
And use my voice

To communicate
My feelings
Accepting my fate
In all my dealings

Be honest and straight
Stick to the facts
Open the floodgate
And brace for the impacts

Ready to walk away
Be courageous and strong
Do not waver and sway
If it is wrong

Too petrified and afraid
To face reality
Disheartened and dismayed
To fight and disagree

Who wants confrontation
And dissension
Leading to castration
And no more attention

But sooner or later
All will come to an end
Bowing to a dictator

Instead of being a friend

Friends listen
Do not judge
Or create divisions
Stonewall without a budge

Who am I talking to
But only to me
I cannot change a view
From another who is free

Revelation

I do not know who you are
You talk three hours through a screen
We did debate and spar
Not ugly or mean

We played with each other
And talked and talked
We enjoyed one another
Our emotions not locked

But what happened that very day
You did not respond or communicate
You replied with nothing to say
Causing me much frustration

You sent a positive message
You missed me as a companion
I thought we had a shot
My plight was not a deep canyon

I raced to see you
To talk to you in person
So much hope to renew
Only to worsen

You would not see me
You would not talk
Address my plea
What a shock

You did not want to come out
And tell me your troubles
And what this was about
My apprehension doubles

Why did you call the night before
Why did we flirt and play
Why did you spend 3 hours on the phone
Why did you act like the good old days

But I learned the reality
You came outside
And said you were free
And your position was clarified

You did not see us long term
You did not want to lead me on
You were very definite and firm
You did not want me as a pawn

It was hard for me to listen
I was denied and rejected
Your tears did glisten
I pleaded and objected

Holding you tight
You were so frail
It was the end of the night
And I took flight

As I drove away
I realized so much

And knew it his way
Our life would be dutch

No more togetherness
No more reliance
No more dependence
No more shared memories

Two lives afloat
In our own little ships
Circling in a moat
On our own trips

The next day I realized
We are good friends
My memories prized
And I wanted to make amends

We can be pals and mates
Open to conversation
Definitely no romantic dates
And no long term relations

We can be kind
And we can be heartfelt
All a matter of the mind
And the cards we are dealt

Friends for life
What does that mean
Not husband and wife
A future unseen

Darkness than Light

Time spent
Time lost
Time went
Time tossed

She was the one
I could love
She was the sun
I write of

Beautiful
Funny
Intelligent
Nurturing

Just as in a day
The sunsets
Everything turns gray
Blackness forgets

The warmth
The laughs
The smiles
The togetherness

You lose your way
You forget the daylight
You wander astray
You take flight

Fly away
Hide away
Stay away
Run away

Less stress
To run and hide
Less mess
Easier on my pride

I am not wrong
I am not mistaken
I am not amiss
I am not wrongheaded

I was slighted
I was insulted
I was uninvited
I was not consulted

Was it necessary
Was it essential
Was it contrary
Was it sequential

No
Not at all
To go toe to toe
And to hit a wall

Now in darkness
Stumbling about

Nothing but starkness
No way out

I am alone
With my thoughts
And a slight moan
My stomach in knots

I will wander
Seeking reality
I will ponder
What is the key

The key to fellowship
The key to friendship
The key to relationship
The key to life

Almost complete
Running out of time
Cannot cheat
Not in my prime

Stumble along
While everyone is asleep
Try to be strong
Do not weep

Understand
After every night
Sun comes to the land
So struggle and fight

Say hello
Wear a smile
Do not judge others
Just love and accept

Ferocious Tide

Why do I grieve
I gave it my all
Rewarded with a reprieve
To stand alone and tall

Reprieve from stress
Walking on eggshells
A game of chess
With no wedding bells

More money
To spend every day
Milk and honey
Spend it my way

Travel the world
Sights to see
Twirl and whirl

I am free

Drugless
My mind works
I must confess
These are perks

Write my rhyming verse
Create and produce thought
I have beaten the curse
No more brain rot

Not drugged dumb
As a mindless ghoul
I have overcome
The ceaseless drool

But is it all that great
To have all this
Without a mate
To hug and kiss

This is why I mourn
I have lost my buddy
Our love torn
My heart muddy

I am so conflicted
So many upsides
I am unrestricted
But a ferocious tide

So may extremes
A passionate obsession
I had so many dreams
And a confession

I miss her
She was unique
A sweet liqueur
An aura of mystique

There will be no one like her

No one to replace our fun
I miss being her chauffeur
But we are done

She sees no need
For a sidekick
Independent and freed
She is her own chick

And this is life
Not very equitable and fair
Without a wonderful wife
And a journey to share

A treacherous fate
To be alone
Which I do hate
Nearing my gravestone

No reason to seek
Another to share
I am past my peak
Along with my wear and tear

Enjoy the positives
And all their good yields
Eliminate the negatives
And their battlefields

Slow down
Stay true
Do not frown

Or turn blue

The easiest way to enjoy
What time is unexpended
Be good and a kind boy
As God intended

Hope and Expectations

Dare I raise my hope
Or raise my expectations
Set me up to be a dope
How about the flirtations

Do I expect her to realize
We are made for each other
And I am better than most guys
Why do I want to bother

To beg her forgiveness
To seek her approval
To deduce her restiveness
To change her disproval

Push her to decide
To spend time with me
Is it mine and her pride
Which is the key

Or is it stupidity
To keep on hoping
When she demonstrates lividity
And I am just coping

I miss our time together
She says the same
How can we tether
Our mutual claim

Leave her alone
Live your life
She has a phone
No more strife

Strife in myself
Strife in her actions
Strife in our childness
Strife in the whole thing

I know we would have fun
We are so good just us
Why does it have to be done
What is the real fuss

I do not know
Questioning her decision
Creating a senseless row
A gigantic collision

She is in control
So let her go
And make some goals
Just go with the flow

Not your best suit
To play it by ear
It might be the best route
Learn to be a seer

Able to visualize
What decisions are best
There may be a prize
If I passed the test

No matter what
My life will be less
But not in a rut
Just some distress

So what is it
Hope that is confused
Expectations that fit
Reconciliation refused

Or is it craziness
To let it rule
Making me melancholy
So stop being a fool

Night to Day

Time Spent
Time lost
Time went
Time tossed

She was the one
I could love
She was the sun
I write of

Beautiful
Funny
Intelligent
Nurturing

Just as in a day
The sunsets
Everything turns gray

Blackness forgets

The warmth
The laughs
The smiles
The togetherness

You lose your way
You forget the daylight
You wander astray
You take flight

Fly away
Hide away
Stay away
Run away

Less stress
To run and hide
Less mess
Easier on my pride

I am not wrong
I am not mistaken
I am not amiss
I am not wrongheaded

I was slighted
I was insulted
I was uninvited
I was not consulted

Was it necessary
Was it essential
Was it contrary
Was it sequential

No
Not at all
To go toe to toe
And to hit a wall

Now in darkness
Stumbling about
Nothing but starkness
No way out

I am alone
With my thoughts
And a slight moan
My stomach in knots

I will wander
Seeking reality
I will ponder
What is the key

The key to fellowship
The key to friendship
The key to relationship
The key to life

Almost complete
Running out of time
Cannot cheat
Not in my prime

Stumble along
While everyone is asleep
Try to be strong
Do not weep

Understand
After every night
Sun comes to the land
So struggle and fight

Say hello
Wear a smile
Do not judge others
Just love and accept

Chapter 7 - My Health

I do not know what is worse? You are getting old, and your physical body is breaking down, or You have pushed yourself so hard that finally, your mental health deteriorates from stress and trauma. Maybe it is both.

For me, I have had both physical and mental issues over the past ten years. I have struggled to feel healthy and to function normally. My first book of poems, [Uplifting Poems About the Death of a Loved One](), discusses and explains my health issues in great detail. Over the past two years, I thought, with Cynthia's help, that I had gotten through the worse part of my illnesses. I was taking Amitriptyline to keep my mental symptoms or crazies under control. The medicine was working, and it still works. Over the past six months, I have had no symptoms, and it has been refreshing.

My physical condition needed constant tweaking to fix my shoes so I could walk as normally as possible. The shoe inserts helped tremendously, and I had less and less pain. If I had any real pain, we would go right to my shoes and readjust the inserts. I was able to maintain a good workout routine. I walked 10,000 steps per day, rode the elliptical for 30 minutes per day, lifted weights daily, and performed yoga two or three times per week. I worked hard to keep exercising because it was the first sign that something serious was wrong.

Overall, I was in good health or a great deal better health until the middle of 2021. I could not breathe anymore. I noticed when I went to the restroom, and I lost my breath. Next, I lost my breath going up the stairs. I went from walking 10,000 steps per day to 0 steps per day. I could not walk the neighborhood without falling out. I could not coach girls softball without having to rest and pace myself. I could not play with Elizabeth and her friends around the house without stopping and breathing hard. Simple work tasks became impossible. The kicker was that I could not play volleyball in the pool with a six-year-old without becoming winded and exhausted. All this occurred in 2 months. I went from exercising daily to not being able to exercise at all.

The doctors have performed many blood tests, X-rays, cat scans, and ultrasounds. I have not had covid, but I have had the covid shots. I await heart cat scans and MRI. These tests will be done in the month of July in 2021.

These poems express how I feel about my medical conditions. I am not scared but annoyed that there is something else wrong with me. These events remind me that life is not fair.

Battle of Nerves vs Medical

What to do next
I wander about
I am perplexed
I want to shout

Leave me alone
Let me be
I want to moan
But then there is she

She is Smart Girl
She will not let me quit
She is a rare precious pearl
She has much grit

You are fine
You are curable
Quit your whine
You are endurable

Your lungs sing a song
Your heart is exceptionally good
Your muscles are strong
You are a forest of maple wood

You fall and almost fall
You have bouts and seasons
Where you hit a wall
Without any reasons

No one has diagnosed you
Telling you anything
No reason to worry and stew
Anxiety and depression sting

Worse than your illness
Quit being an awful bore
Live each day in its brilliance
Open the morning door and roar

Life is noble and grand
Life is pleasing and sweet
Life is unexplored land
Life is a delicious treat

Smart Girl wants to pursue
Conversion disorder and
Functional neurological disorder
Which is fine with me

The brain and nervous mechanisms
Do not efficiently communicate
Resulting in many schisms
In my neurological state

Somewhere between nerves and mental
Everyone knows I am crazy
But let us not be judgmental
We all can be a little hazy

Good news I believe
Continue the medical journey

Looking for reprieve
After six years of a debilitating tourney

What is a year or two more
Smart Girl motivates me
To continue the unfair war
And I agree

The Drug

Amitriptyline
Is my drug
Not really crystalline
I think like a slug

So very very dragging
So very very hampered
So very very lagging
So very very hammered

I cannot think
I cannot write
I cannot read
I cannot understand

I can walk
I can talk
I can exercise
I can drive

A trade off
Lose the crazy woes
Do not unbelieve or scoff
Or live in the shadows

Easier to be alone
Easier to hideaway
Easier to be my own
Easier to live that way

Live in solitary
Or to fight the darkness
I am my adversary
What a starkness

To live in society
Amitriptyline is required
To end anxiety
A new life is desired

Slow with limited derailments
Sleep too much
Drugged but no aliments
Amitriptyline is a crutch

Last time 10 mg

Then 20 and 30 mg
Then 40 to 70 mg
All the way to 80 mg

In the end
It began shirking
No more dividends
And it quit working

Better for a while
To have some assistance
A pleasant smile
And a healthy existence

It is the Season

Be jolly
Be happy
Be melancholy
Be crappie

Emotions uncontrolled
Emotions high and low
Emotions lukewarm to cold
Emotions surge and flow

What triggers this crap
What triggers these emotions
What triggers in a snap
What triggers these commotions

I do not know for sure
There is no rhyme or reason
There is no sure cure
There are just seasons

Seasons of no complaints
Seasons of quiet and peace
Seasons of no restraints
Seasons like a chess piece

King full of power and authority
Queen doing all that I please
Knight jumping over and around
Pawn taking small baby steps

All these pieces have a role
Roles in different seasons
Seasons in and out of control
I do not know the reasons

All I can do is believe
Believe in God
Believe in rest and reprieve
Believe I am flawed and odd

I have a limitations
I have wants and needs
I have troubled relations
I have good and bad deeds

What does that make me
Odd or distressed
Or a human being free
Refreshed and blessed

Glad and fortunate
All that I have today
I make no argument
Attitude is the way

Not vitamins
Not supplements
Not exercise
Not diet

How you see life
How you react

How you handle strife
How you handle facts

Can you handle stress
Ups and downs
All the fess and mess
All the sights and sounds

I do not know
But live in peace
Go with the flow
Accept the decrease

Everyone cannot be kings
Or queens
Or sprout wings
Or have good genes

But everyone can be
Nice
Kind
Tolerant

Not rude
Irritable
Causing an endless feud
Or endless hating

Just Write

No more mind drug
No more captivity
No more a slug
No more inactivity

I can think and write
There are ideas and activity
My mind is clear and bright
I have vision and creativity

What satisfaction
A few words in print
My words have interaction
Now I am on a sprint

Create a poem every day
For long as it lasts
And a long time I pray
But there are no complex forecasts

Maybe restart my novel
It is all in my head
I will not fall apart and grovel
Just forge ahead

I am optimistic about my ability
I know what I want to generate
I have so many possibilities
I have to accept my fate

Just create a rhyme
And let them grow
Let the words climb
Creating a sweet flow

Doctors

Where do I begin
Do I cuss or do I praise
Sin or take it on the chin
Doctors run me through a maze

No way out just lost
Lost and fumbling
And there is a horrible cost
I am just tumbling

Down in the pit of sorrow
Down in the pit of despair
Down in the pit of loneliness
Down in the pit of misery

Do the doctors care
All forty eight of them
Not from my armchair
But they are not scum

And it may not be their fault
My problem is complicated
Everything needs a grain of salt
And it has to be debated

You fall backwards right
Yes and light hurts
You are sensitive to light
And it takes a bit until it reverts

What is it we wonder
We do not have a clue
Was there blunder
And that was their view

Wait until it manifests itself
Then we will know
And pick it right off the shelf
Just keep your life in escrow

Not only Mayo Clinic
But Vanderbilt too
I became a cynic
Not believing their doo doo

Fall backwards was googled
And what appeared

Progressive Supranuclear Palsy
That was really weird
But only diagnosed with an autopsy

What in the world is this
And how do I know
I cannot just ignore it and dismiss
If I am part of this game show

Am I lucky to be a contestant
In some weird rare disease
Not cured with a decongestant
There is no cure to put you at ease

What are the facts
Let me count them one by one
And see if this is the way my body acts
I might hit a few home runs

Light sensitive falling backward sore neck
Lean backwards close my eyes blurred vision
Brain fog brain locks up forget words
Mispronounce words cannot say words

Disequilibrium unsteady visual complaints burning eyes
difficulties in looking up or down slowness of thought
impaired memory personality changes in mood
sleeping problems agitation irritable and depression

I won the game the league championship and series

I had all the symptoms but swallowing bladder and
raising eyelids
But what do I know because it is only a theory
Diagnosis your symptoms the medical community
forbids

There is no cure if you ask
But you look too good to be sick
You are not ready for a death mask
Not parkinsonian or using a walking stick

Nope you are healthy good and fine
Just a few nervous anxious tics
You are a long way from a decline
Believe nothing is wrong and that is the fix

Many believe these stupid falsehoods
It is not their only precious life
And let me sell you a bill of goods
There will always be strife

After you cannot physically move
Doctors will confirm oh yes indeed you have PSP
One or two years to die not to improve
I guess it is all about me whoopee

My Heart

My heart hurts
Was it love
Or too many desserts
Or God from above

Does it matter
Why I cannot take a breath
My heart goes pitter patter
Along the path to my death

How did I get here
After exercising too much
Did I cause too much wear
Or is this a crutch

Did I eat the wrong food
Mostly salads and meat
Pizza when in the mood
Along with something sweet

Ice cream and cake
Cookie dough with glaze
Maybe a shake
I did graze

Food or exercise
The doctors do not know
I wonder if they are wise
Or trying to collect dough

Test after test
What do they show
Nothing in my chest
Maye my heart flow

More tests and protocols
To see if my veins are clear
Just wait for our calls
And keep a good cheer

Sometimes it is hard
To be enthusiastic
When you cannot walk the yard
Or anything too drastic

I cannot breathe when I piss
I cannot breathe climbing up the stairs
I cannot breathe to walk the block
I cannot breathe playing in the pool

These are not drastic actions
And it is very tough
No to have reactions
When I cannot get a puff of air

I walked 10000 steps daily
I lifted weights daily
I used the elliptical for 30 minutes daily
I performed yoga every two days

What happened to me
Will it go away

Can they fix this stuff
Or keep it at bay

I do wonder
Can it be fixed
Or do I go under
My thoughts are mixed

Issues upon issues
Troubles upon troubles
Stress upon stress
Anxiety upon anxiety

Thinking can be worse
Worrying for naught
Or is this a curse
And I got caught

Or is it a side effect
Of a Covid shot
Is there a connect
Throwing it all in the pot

Heart inflammation
They do say
Maybe a causation
To take me astray

My shot in late March
My condition sometime in April
Is there a connecting arch
Or is this gossip or a fable

Chapter 8 - My Fourth Quarter

The fourth quarter is the most critical time of football games. The last quarter is where comebacks are made, or letdowns exaggerated by poor play and attitudes. Football teams who lose have forgotten. They forgot and did not understand what it will take to win. They do not know how much time is left in the game, they do not execute, realizing first downs, and they did not march down the field to score.

Life is like a football game. We have lived the first three-quarters of our lives, knowing our lives will be more challenging in the end. In the fourth quarter, we will face money problems, face relationship issues, face physical limitations, and face mental troubles. Just like the football game, why do we not execute? Why did we not prepare? Why did we not know how much time do we have left?

Most likely, we never thought it was going to happen to me. I never thought I would have health issues for ten years throughout my fifties. I did not believe that I would be single at 59 years old. I felt that I was a good catch and a wonderful person.

I can mope and feel sorry for myself, or I can execute a plan to start a new journey. I can dream of a new path to cope with my limitations and strive for a new life.

The poems in this chapter will explore my expectations for the future. I feel there is a great future for me waiting for me. I have to want it and to get it. These verses will describe my motivation to experience a remarkable life after sixty.

End of Game

I have been there
Struggling to win
Throwing up a prayer
Taking it on the chin

A strong punch
I worked so hard
And I feel the crunch
My soul and body marred

As in the game
So many opportunities
To win with fame
For our communities

But it is not finished
You may feel it is
Do not be diminished
Or end with a fizz

Take stock in your abilities
And know you are strong
Reduce your liabilities
And sing a happy song

There is more time to comeback
Life has not ended
Pushback and attack
Everything will be splendid

Remember your durability
And your unique traits
Hopefulness is not unnecessary futility
But a date with our fates

Decide to fight
For your hereafter
The day is bright
Sunny with laughter

React to your circumstances
Enjoy the here and now
Take your chances
Stay behind the plow

Make your rows straight
A strenuous chore
No time to wait
You can score

Fall Apart

Can this dream fall apart
My health can abort
When I depart
So be a good sport

Make sure you do not die
Clear up the questions
Something is awry
I am waiting for suggestions

Test upon test
Not your lungs
No breath when pressed
Doctors speak in tongues

I cannot understand
Their medical mumbo jumbo
Or where I stand
I am not Colombo

A detective from the past
Who solved all his cases
After sixty minutes have passed
Winning all his races

My race is not a television show
It is an actual life event
Doctors do not know
What is my torment

Two more tests
And I will be done
No more pests
Get ready to run

Run to your aspirations
Run to your fantasies
Run to your future
Run to your dreams

Be unhurried
All will be good
Stay unworried
All will be understood

Never Too Late

I understand it is late
To start something new
But why wait
To make a breakthrough

Your mind will intercept you
Stopping you from pursuing
Any new thing or worldview
It will take some coercing

How to change
To get the courage
You must exchange
Discourage to encourage

Encourage yourself
To look at your strengths
Take them off the shelf

Go to any lengths

To find a new way
A life changing journey
No reason to stay
Join the tourney

Seek opportunities
To explore and venture
Foreign communities
To find adventure

Istanbul
Black Sea
Via Egnatia
Phillippi

Places of history
Inspirations to seek
A past mystery
Very unique

Chasing this storyline
Requires sacrifice
A resilient spine
And a price

Is it worth the chase
To leave this place
Pack your suitcase
Accept and embrace

You will die here
Frustrated and senile

Or you can hear
The cry for a new lifestyle

Epilogue

After I finished this book of poetry, it has become an exceedingly difficult time for me. I do not know where I am going or what direction I will travel. I cannot breathe. If I do anything to exert myself, I lose all my breath from using the restroom to walking the neighborhood. I have to stop and keel over to get my breath. This is a complete shock to me because I was walking 10,000 steps per day, riding the elliptical for 30 minutes per day, lifting weights every day, and participating in yoga 2 or 3 times per week.

The medical community is performing tests, but it is a waiting game while they schedule one more test after the last one did not reveal any issues. I feel that I have traveled from one series of doctors dealing with many issues outlined in my first book of poems to another series of doctors dealing with this breathing or heart issue.

Over the next 30 to 60 days, the doctors have upped their game. They plan to look at my heart using cat scans, dye, and MRI. No stress test because I did one three years ago. I quickly passed 10 minutes uphill. I hope these new tests reveal why I cannot breathe.

About the Author

Conrad Birmingham

Conrad Birmingham is a businessman who is retired, and he is trying to stay busy. He has no real talent at writing any type of writing except Quality Assurance Programs, Business Plans, Bible Study Notes, Business Price Quotes, Business Memos, Loan Requests, Consulting Reports, and all things business.

He has written poems for the past fifteen years. He has written two books of poems and he hopes you will enjoy reading them.

Conrad likes four stanzas with rhyming verses. They are called Quatrains, but he does not really care. They are poems with four lines that rhyme. Also, he does not like punctuation. He does not use punctuation, allowing the verses to flow as they flow. He wants the reader to figure it out, and there are no participation trophies here.

He hopes you enjoy his writings, and he wishes for you to visit his website and Facebook pages. He would like for you to leave comments and reviews. He encourages you to ask him questions about his writings. Good or bad, he does not mind. He wants to get better at writing, and he believes the best way is to be criticized and pushed to be better.

Books By the Author

Uplifting Poems About the Death of a Loved One

Uplifting Poems About the Death of a Loved One is a journey of my life, especially in the last five years. I have struggled through medical issues for these five years, including depression and anxiety. I am challenged with the belief that I have a disease that is not diagnosed, and I am going to die. True or not true, that is what I believe. He first book of poems works up to this obsession with death. The book of poems ends with hope.

Conrad Birmingham: Mini-book with My Seekers- Help Me Believe Lessons, Blog Posts, Poems, Novels and Mini-Book Writings

I have consolidated all of my writing in this book. This book is an anthology of my creative work including blogs, poems, and Bible studies.

Made in the USA
Columbia, SC
19 July 2021